**COW NECK PENINSULA HISTORICAL SOCIETY**

# WWI

## THE HOMEFRONT

### OUR COMMUNITY TAKES ACTION

**FARMERETTE**

**REGIMENT**

**SUFFRAGETTE**

**On the cover:**

**Top:**

A member of the Port Washington Home Guard in front of Locust Grove Pavilion, Port Washington, c. 1917.

**Three photos at bottom, left to right:**

Farmerettes on the back of a wagon.

The Port Washington Home Guard mustering at Main Street School.

The Port Washington Suffragists marching in the 1913 Firemen's Parade in front of what is now Finn McCool's; (Photo: Landis Valley Village & Farm Museum, Pennsylvania Historical & Museum Commission.)

Copyright 2022
Cow Neck Peninsula Historical Society
All rights reserved
ISBN #979-8-218-01871-9

## Exhibition and Catalogue Contributors

**Joan DeMeo Lager,** Curatorial Director & Author

**Betty Mintz,** Exhibition & Catalogue Art Director

**Christopher Bain,** Photography Director & Exhibition Installation

**Jennifer Wiggins**, Researcher

| | | |
|---|---|---|
| Rachel Bialer | William Evans | Morgan Nelson |
| Fred Blumlein | Christine Izzo | Peggy Podstupka |
| Kaitlin Caginalp | Margot Gramer | Barbara Silbert |
| Elayne Cashdan | Tessa Jordan | Marion Staszak |
| Lynne Chrapliwy | Robert Lager | Gilda Tesoriero |
| Lucy Davidson | Ross Lumpkin | Maz Troppe |
| | Susan Murphy | |

## Our Mission

The mission of the Cow Neck Peninsula Historical Society is to engage people of all ages in programs that highlight the lifestyles of the people and families that lived and worked on our peninsula throughout the years. Central to this mission is the preservation of the Sands-Willets House (circa 1735) and the Thomas Dodge Homestead (circa 1721), which the Society operates as house-museums, serving as resources for the community.

## Board of Directors

**Christopher Bain**, President

**Marla Freeman,** 1st Vice President, Art Director

**Katherine Crean**, 2nd Vice President

**Kenneth J. Buettner,** Treasurer

**Betty Mintz,** Recording Secretary

| | | |
|---|---|---|
| Lee Aitken | Robert Lager | Jay Stone |
| Linn Johnson | Ross Lumpkin | Colin Wiggins |
| Tessa Jordan | Jon Ruvio | Jennifer Wiggins |

Artist: Childe Hassam, The Fourth of July, 1916 (The Greatest Display of the American Flag Ever Seen in New York, Climax of the Preparedness Parade in May). Oil on Canvas. 36 x 26 1/8 in. Gift of Richard Gilder, 2016. New-York Historical Society, 2016.31.

This Exhibition is dedicated to

James & Karli Hagedorn

*with our grateful thanks for their ongoing generous support*

*of our Educational Programming*

With our sincere thanks to

**Robert David Lion Gardiner Foundation**

*Printing and binding of the Exhibition Catalogue*

**Bank of America**

*Printing of the Exhibition Graphic Panels*

The Evening Telegram, New York, July 20, 1917

## Table of Contents

| | |
|---|---:|
| Introduction | **9** |
| Why Did the United States Enter WWI? | **14** |
| Civilians to Soldiers | **24** |
| Farmerettes | **48** |
| The War Effort | **66** |
| In Our Spare Time... | **80** |
| The Women Who Served | **96** |
| The Men Who Served | **110** |
| An Army of Animals | **132** |
| Suffragettes | **140** |

# BEWARE
## — OF —
# FEMALE SPIES

Women are being employed by the enemy to secure information from Navy men, on the theory that they are less liable to be suspected than male spies. Beware of inquisitive women as well as prying men.

**SEE EVERYTHING
HEAR EVERYTHING
SAY NOTHING**
Concerning any matter bearing upon the work of the Navy

## SILENCE IS SAFETY

## Introduction

This catalogue reflects our exhibition's focus on Port Washington and other Long Island communities' response to World War I by establishing active homefronts. We show how we lived, changed lifestyles and were shaped by the war effort. We also examine how individual and societal change was achieved. We discuss how history repeats itself by exploring women's rights, the rights of African Americans and the 1918 flu pandemic, as well as politics and propaganda. But to understand the impact of World War I on Port Washington, one must have a general idea of what was happening across the country.

. . .

A month after Germany declared war in Europe in 1914, German sabotage in our country began. The German Diplomatic Corps network attacked sites that sold supplies to the Allies. Many of the locations were in New Jersey; over 200 fires and explosions occurred along the East Coast. A DuPont gunpowder plant on a mountain slope in New Jersey was blown up, jolting the terrain like an earthquake. The massive blast was so powerful that it was felt in four states. In August of 1914 the New York City Police Commissioner found it necessary to create a bomb squad.

One of the largest explosions, measuring 5.5 on the Richter scale, was on Black Tom Island in New York Harbor. It was determined in 1939 that Imperial Germany was responsible. Reparations of $95 million were agreed upon in 1953, and the payments were finally completed in 1979. This act of terrorism was partially responsible for the creation of domestic intelligence agencies and the passage of the 1917 Espionage Act.

Anti-German propaganda increased following all of the industrial sabotage – bombings, fires, and sinking of cargo ships, fishing vessels, and even passenger ships, such as the British ocean liner, the RMS Lusitania, killing 1,198 passengers and crew. German-Americans faced suspicion, and German language classes and German newspapers all closed their doors or were shut down. As frankfurters became "hot dogs" and sauerkraut became "liberty cabbage," our government registered 250,000 German immigrants and required them to carry ID cards.

The immigrants from Central Power countries (the German Empire, the Austro-Hungarian Empire, the Ottoman Empire, and the Kingdom of Bulgaria), numbering over 10 million in the 1910 census, faced this discrimination as well. At Detroit's Ford factory, with workers of 53 nationalities speaking more than 100 languages and dialects, management faced difficulty assigning men to tasks. They had to carefully segregate men to ensure that fights did not break out between those from Central Power countries and the neighboring Allied countries (Great Britain, France, Russia, and Romania.)

Two German submarines, U-boats 151 and 156, crossed the Atlantic in 1916 to the still neutral United States. Their vessels had sufficient range to make the passage, and they put their month-long sea capabilities to work attacking our shipping. They laid mines, cut the telegraph cables between New York City and Nova Scotia, and sank fishing schooners and took their crews prisoner. On June 2, 1918, a day that became known as "Black Sunday," in just a few hours the Germans sank 6 ships and damaged more. The pirating continued throughout the summer months along the eastern shores of the U.S.

U-151 went on to New York Harbor and then laid underwater mines in the shipping lanes off the Long Island coast south of Fire Island. U-156 went to Cape Cod, wreaking similar havoc. In Maine, another 34 fishing boats were sunk. Our seaplanes and Navy submarine chasers responded but to no avail. The Germans then resumed unrestricted warfare in the Atlantic, resulting in the sinking of hundreds of our ships by the end of the war.

In response to rumors that the U-boats were equipped with aircraft, anti-aircraft defenses were set up in New York City. The Massachusetts State House had its gold dome painted over to reduce the risk of bombing.

Pro-war feelings grew. So did anti-war protests. Some opponents of U.S. involvement in the growing European conflict would agree to fight for American rights, but not for Europe's. Others were totally against our taking part. In Baltimore, on the eve of our declaration of war, a speaker in favor of peace was mobbed by 1,000 pro-war supporters. Then the pro-peace supporters sang our National Anthem, causing the patriotic pro-war supporters to stand at attention, allowing the speaker to slip away. But it wasn't always that easy.

The country remained divided after our declaration of war. Propaganda was widely used in a variety of forms to rally an isolationist nation into supporting the war. Posters were a popular and effective form which utilized various techniques to inspire or shame people into complying with the needs of the government, be it for military support, for food, or to raise funds for the war effort.

Wartime propaganda was prevalent in the schools, and misrepresentations of the truth were incorporated into numerous study plans. A partisan informative bulletin was dispensed by the Committee on Public Information, in conjunction

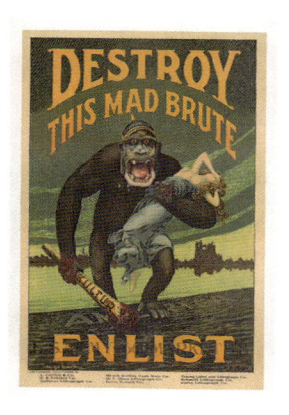

Innocents in Lusitania sinking, by Fred Spear, 1915.

German barbarian arriving on our shores, by Harry Ryle Hopps, 1917.

Men's masculinity at stake, by Laura Brey, poster contest winner, 1917.

with the Secretaries of State, War, and Navy, whose intent was to sway the American people into supporting the war using an emotional appeal. 75,000 "Four-Minute Men," selected from the local communities, recited a prepared speech in a variety of venues for the four minutes it took to change the reel in the movie theatres. They encouraged the townspeople to become enthused about backing the war and supporting the views the government wanted heard.

Many socialists had come to the United States because of President Wilson's stance against war, and the Socialist Party now rallied vehemently against war. As a result, over a dozen socialist publications, one with a circulation of over a half million, were banned by the postal service, damaging the strength of the party.

The Espionage Act was enacted in June 1917 and suppressed any unpatriotic comment, treasonous or not. Government authorities issued $10,000 fines and 20 year prison terms for interfering with the military in wartime and $5,000 fines and 5 year prison terms for using mail against regulations. Postal inspectors mistreated owners of German-American publications, exaggerated minor violations, and had German-Americans placed in internment camps. 4,000 were detained in 1917-1918, some for espionage and some for being pro-Germany. Beatings, tarring and feathering, and even lynching of German-Americans took place in the United States.

Under the Espionage Act, the offices of the International Workers of the World were raided in 3 states, and 166 members were convicted. Vigilante groups attacked them, including at the Tulsa Outrage, where a black-robed group of the KKK tarred and feathered men for not owning war bonds. An Ohio clergyman addressing a peace meeting was bound and gagged and whipped to near death.

The conflict between anti- and pro- war supporters in the country kept growing. The President was unable to bring about any mitigating change, and his command was becoming unmanageable. Postmaster General Albert Burleson wanted to wield even greater powers, and the Trading with the Enemy Act provided him that opportunity. Before long, foreign newspapers and editorials had to be approved, and a skipped issue could result in a loss of monthly status, causing mailings to be stopped altogether.

Attorney General Thomas Watt Gregory had his say too. He felt that legal procedures protected the guilty and that mob violence was effective in attaining justice. His heavy-handed tactics and extralegal scrutiny led to judges and attorneys being reprimanded for adhering to their regular practices. He and Postmaster General Burleson felt that the Espionage Act was not restrictive enough, so they fostered the enactment of the Sedition Act. Among other provisions, the act made it illegal to speak or write anything detrimental about the military, the government, the flag, or the Constitution.

President Wilson's actions allowed the erosion of many such basic rights and let narrow men destroy his base. Freedom of speech, common decency, truth in education, and racial policies all suffered and continued even after the war. Disenchantment and disillusion prevailed for many.

Long-standing racial prejudices continued. The Wilson administration did not allow the African American Divisions, that had served so heroically in the war, to march with the white soldiers in the victory parades in France. The 369th Division returned to New York City as heroes and had a spectacular victory parade. Travelling to the south, however, they found segregated communities where Jim Crow laws ruled. Segregation, ostracism, and lynching continued. The North also presented difficulties to the returning African American soldiers due to overcrowding from the Great Migration northward during the war. The same efforts were not made for returning Black soldiers who needed jobs as for white soldiers. The acceptance that many of the Black soldiers had found in France was difficult to forsake on their return home, sowing yet more seeds for unrest and for civil rights movements.

The sheer magnitude of the Influenza Pandemic of 1918 seemed unimaginable before 2019, and yet after our experience with the Covid-19 pandemic, it tragically seems more familiar.

The Spanish Flu pandemic continued for several years and included at least 4 waves. 16 million died worldwide from World War I, but 150 million people died worldwide from the 1918 Pandemic, with 675,000 dying in the United States alone.

People masked, they quarantined when ill, walked in fresh air when they could, and staggered their work hours. Schools and businesses were shut down when necessary. In 1918, the New York Telephone Company asked the public to refrain from making unnecessary calls because so many operators were out with the flu and medical calls were not getting through. The public complied quickly. It is likely they would have welcomed a vaccine and antibiotics, but there were none.

Women, who had served wholeheartedly, both in our country and overseas, had not yet secured the right to vote by the war's end. It took more work by women, who were split in their viewpoints; some had supported the war while putting their fight for woman suffrage aside, and some had continued their fight for suffrage.

> *"The right of citizens of the United States to vote shall not be denied or abridged by the United States or by any State on account of sex.*
>
> *Congress shall have power to enforce this article by appropriate legislation."*

In 1875, Susan B. Anthony and Elizabeth Cady Stanton had written these words, presented to Congress in 1878 and every year thereafter. 41 years later on August 18, 1920, they were approved by Congress.

## A Word of Appreciation

When the influenza epidemic was at its height, so many of our operators were absent that it was impossible to handle promptly all the telephone calls that were offered.

Knowing that a word of explanation to the New York public would relieve the situation, we stated our case and asked our patrons to assist us by restricting their use of the telephone to *necessary* calls.

The response, as was expected, was immediate. Citizens' associations of all kinds, individual users both large and small, public telephone agents, in fact all classes of the telephone-using public gave us splendid cooperation.

This help was given cheerfully and willingly and the inconveniences were accepted with a good humor that greatly cheered those operators who were working so ably to carry the load during the absence of their fellow-workers.

While many of our operators are still away and some restriction is still necessary on the general use of the telephone, the worst of a bad situation is now passed and we take this opportunity of expressing our appreciation of your kindly help.

*THANK YOU!*

NEW YORK TELEPHONE COMPANY

. . .

Catastrophic events and social movements affect the entire country, the important, and the powerful, but they also affect the individual man, woman, and child. In our exhibit we will explore how the people of Port Washington and Long Island responded to these world events.

14    WWI: The Homefront • Regiment • Cow Neck Peninsula Historical Society

# Why Did the United States Enter WWI?

President Woodrow Wilson won reelection on November 7, 1916 with the slogan, "He kept us out of the war."

Less than five months later, he asked Congress to declare war on Germany.

# A Controversial Climate

April 2, 1917: That afternoon police were repelling pacifists trying to gain entry into the Capitol. That evening, the President entered the Capitol to address Congress. He asserted that Germany had already been warring against us, many times over, and it was time to make a decision:

*"There is one choice we cannot make, we are incapable of making. We will not choose the path of submission…"*

"At the word 'submission,' Chief Justice White with an expression of joy and thankfulness on his face…raised his hands high in the air, and brought them together with a heartfelt bang; and House, Senate, and galleries followed him with a roar like a storm. It was a cheer so deep and so intense and so much from the heart that it sounded like a shouted prayer." – Special to The New York Times, Washington, April 2

We will now take a look at the escalating sabotage on our shores that led to our entry into the war.

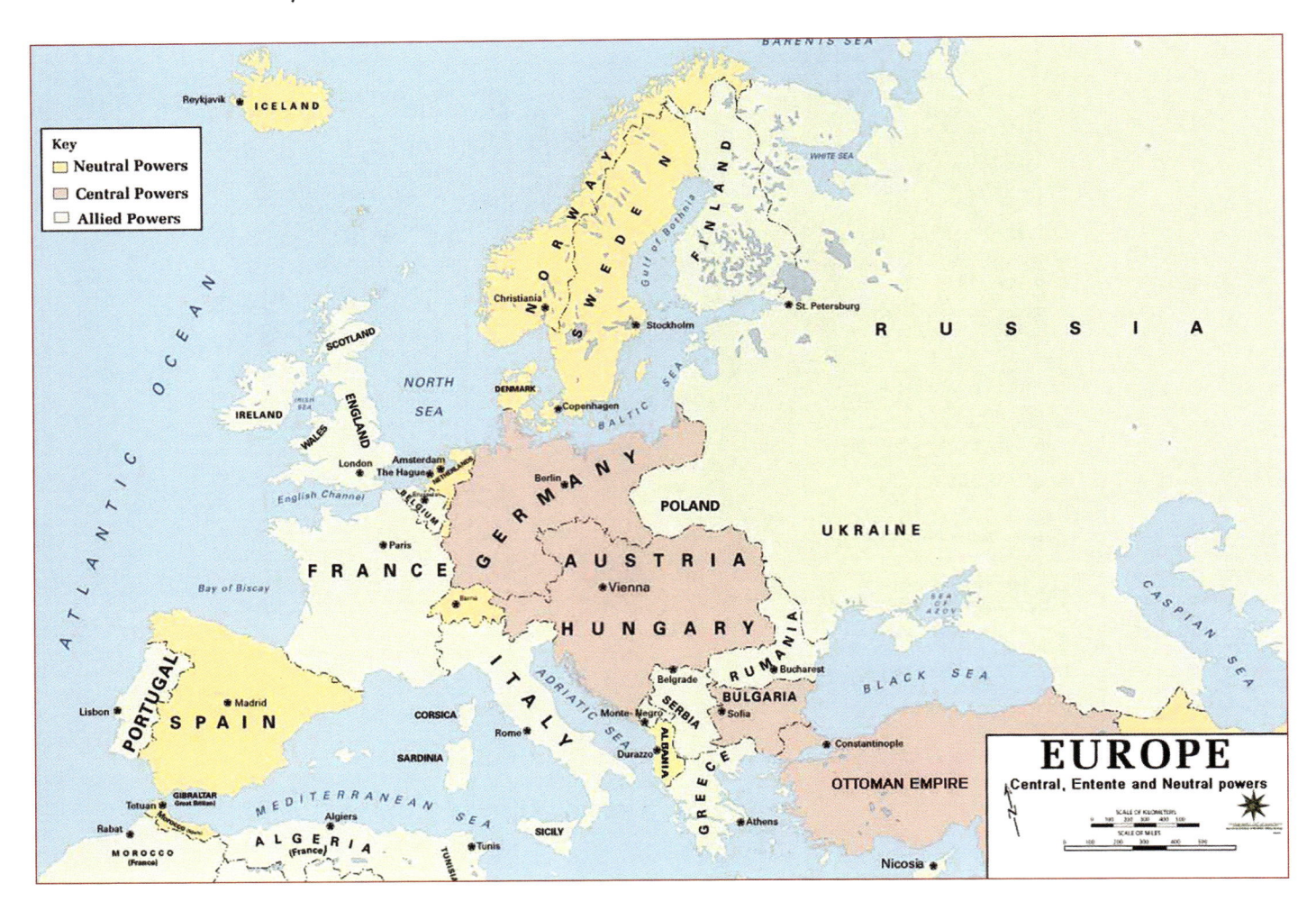

# 1914

**June 28: It All Started With an Assassination!**
Austro-Hungarian Archduke Franz Ferdinand and wife Sophie, killed by Serbian.

**July 28: The Great War Begins!**
Austria-Hungary attacked Serbia. Germany invaded neighbors.

# 1915

**January 11: Explosions in New Jersey!**
Over 200 industrial explosions start, felt in 6 states, seen from NYC skyscrapers, $2+M damage (1915 $)

**April 22: Germans Gas Allies in France!**
160 tons of chlorine in 5,730 cylinders were released as green clouds in the first use of chemical warfare.

**May 7: German U-boat Sinks Lusitania!**
Killed 1,198; 128 Americans. German sub warfare restricted. Did British protection fail so Americans would enter war?

**December 3: German Attachés are Saboteurs!**
President Wilson expelled all German attachés.

**Left:** A suspicious fire broke out in Port Newark, NJ at a government reservation with base, 4500' pier, and plans for building 150 steel ships.

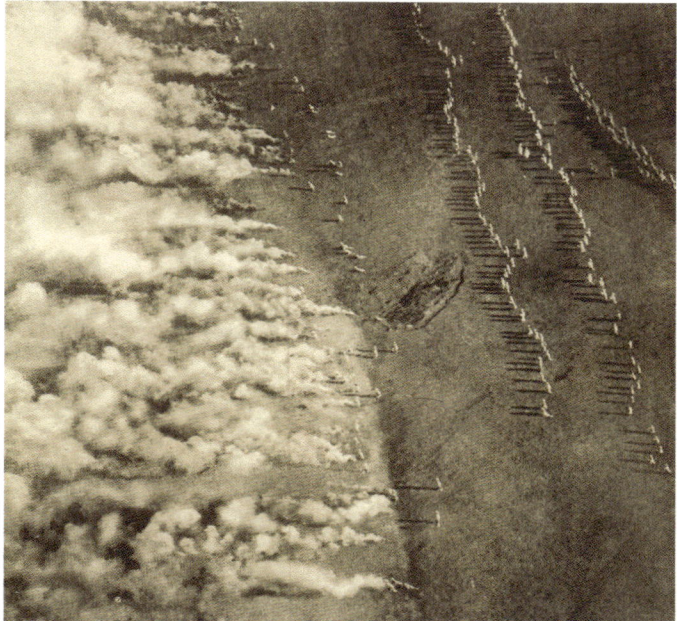

**Above:** Germans in the center have just released poisonous gas. 3 lines of Germans are awaiting the order to charge. Photo by Russian aviator.

**Left:** Lusitania victims being buried in mass grave in Queenston, Ontario, Canada, on May 10th. In foreground, American Helen Smith, unaware she lost her parents, two siblings, and aunt.

WWI: The Homefront • Regiment • Cow Neck Peninsula Historical Society

# 1916

**January 29: Virginia's Anthrax Lab Disbanded!**
New York police located German agents killing thousands of horses meant for Allies.

**July 30: Black Tom Explosions in N.Y. Harbor!**
Munitions depot blown up. Richter scale 5.5, shook states, NYC windows shattered. Lady Liberty's shrapnel halted torch tours. 13 warehouses, 100+ railroad cars, more, gone.

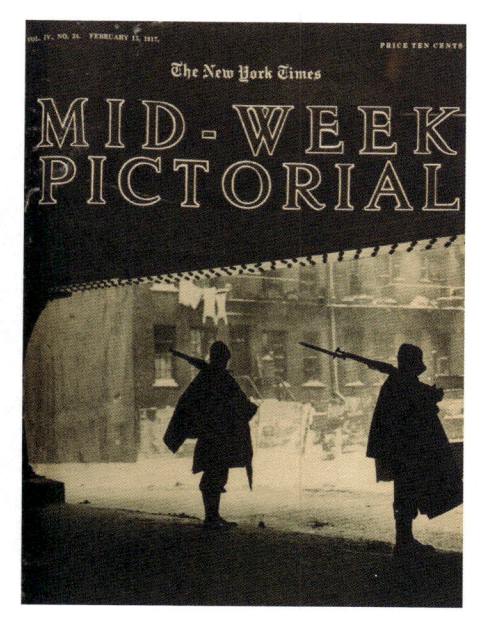

**Above:** Black Tom Island after explosion showing flattened warehouses. Black Tom Island is west of Ellis Island and the Statue of Liberty and is now in Liberty State Park.

**Left:** New York Naval Militiamen guarding the piers of the Brooklyn Bridge from possible damage by bombs.

**Left, bottom:** Guarding the Hudson River where seized German ships were berthed.

**Right:** Tenth Infantry on patrol near Valley Stream. Quarters in Lynbrook water works station, men taking shifts.

# 1917

**February 1: Germany Resumes Sub Warfare!**
Germans: Americans unprepared for war. Sank British ships daily, American ships monthly.

**February 3: U.S. Cuts Ties with Germany!**
President Wilson wanted to arm merchant ships; Senate said no. Wilson armed them by executive order, citing old anti-piracy law.

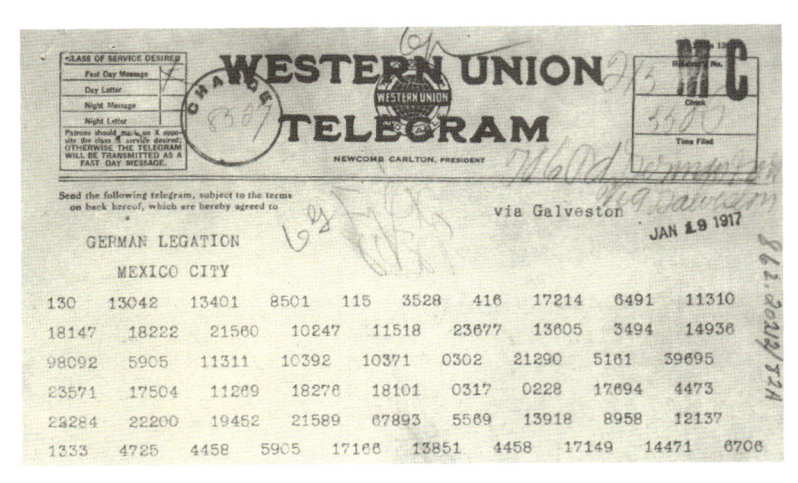

**March 1: U.S. Told of Zimmermann Telegram!**
Germany asked Mexico to declare war on U.S. in exchange for Texas, New Mexico, Arizona. British quiet to keep from Germans that they had broken the code.

**April: Germans Sinking Allied Shipping!**
British hungry, UK grain at 6 week end; long lines for coal, sugar, potatoes. Germans starving.

**April 6: U.S. Declares War on Germany!**
Americans harshly divided in pro-/anti- war viewpoints. Government propaganda issued to rally country.

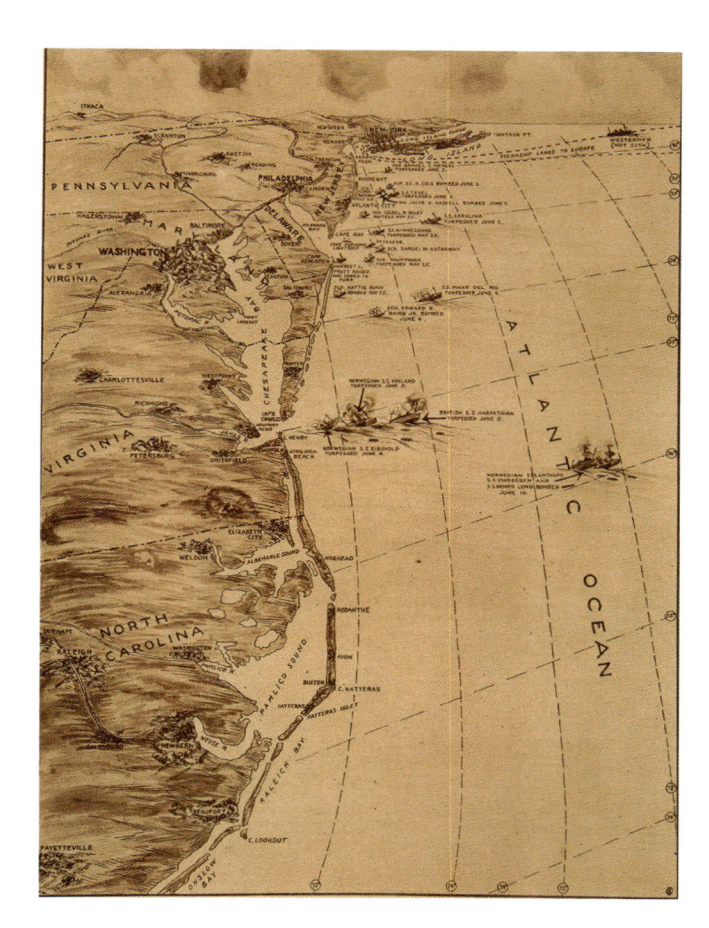

**Left, top:** The Germans were sinking Allied and neutral ships off our East Coast.

**Right:** German super-submarine U-58 in Newport Harbor, R.I. before a spate of ships were sunk in the area.

## WAR DECLARED!

The sabotage that had begun a month after the Archduke's assassination in 1914 continued to grow in intensity with each passing year. Americans were angry, and pro-war sentiment had grown. Yet Wilson had been reelected to "keep us out of the war," and there were anti-war protests and peace marches. But war was now declared, and our community chose to support our soldiers and the country as best as it could.

WWI: The Homefront • Regiment • Cow Neck Peninsula Historical Society

24   WWI: The Homefront • Regiment • Cow Neck Peninsula Historical Society

# Civilians to Soldiers

**"Somewhere in France on active service with the American Expeditionary Forces, August 22nd, 1918"**

"I am on my way back to the front line…have been a few days in the base hospital, for I was gassed on August 7, but not bad enough to affect my lungs or throat. It did, however, put my eyes out of business for three days…Well, Pop…don't let Ma worry, for I am all right…"

—**Private Joseph S. Allen, Co. B 305th Infantry**, to his father, Game Protector Thomas Allen, The Port Washington News, October 4, 1918

# Home Guard

On April 4, 1917, as America was about to enter the war, Port Washington held a spirited meeting in Liberty Hall on Carlton Avenue to form their own home defense force. Over 200 men volunteered for twice weekly drills at Main Street School. Leaders with military training turned the group into a well-disciplined, smartly uniformed force that became known as one of the best trained in the state. All its men who later enlisted were immediately made corporal.

**Top**: One of the three company captains training Port's volunteers at Main Street School.

**Three photos**: The Port Washington Home Guard at its encampment next to Locust Grove Pavilion.

WWI: The Homefront • Regiment • Cow Neck Peninsula Historical Society

HEADQUARTERS HOME GUARD
PORT WASHINGTON

ORDERS,  
No. 1.  }  May 4, 1917.

I. The Executive Committee having appointed the undersigned Commanding officer of the Military Division of the Home Defense League, he hereby assumes command.

II. The following appointments are announced:
Company A. Capt. J. J. Floherty.
   Lieut. Wm. R. Benét.
Company B. Capt. F. T. Lyons.
   Lieut. P. J. White.
Company C. Capt. Henry Eagle.
   Lieut. Philander Norton.
   First Sergt. C. M. Wysong.
Surgeon, Dr. L. A. Newman.
They will be respected and obeyed accordingly.
Sergeant Irving Sands is detailed from Co. C as acting Quartermaster.
Donald Ross is appointed Scout orderly to the Major.

III. Regular Company and Battalion drills are ordered until further notice, on Wednesdays at 8 P.M. and Sundays at 9 A.M. on the High-school grounds. Should the weather be inclement, the men will assemble in the High-school building. On Sundays, men will be excused at 10.30, who so notify the Captain of their desire to fall out.
Action has been taken to equip the men with regulation uniforms. All who feel inclined to pay for the outfit ($7.50 for hat, coat, trousers and leggins) may do so, and own the uniform outright. The others will understand that the uniform is loaned to them only as long as they are on time to answer roll call, and perform 75% of the drills and other duty. Men who fall below that average, will be required to turn in the uniform to the Quartermaster, and allow some one else to have it that can perform full duty. The appropriation for the uniform fund is limited, and the officers will use their discretion, as to who are entitled to them.

IV. The ladies of the "Village Welfare Society" have kindly volunteered to present an American flag, so that the Battalion may have "Colors", on occasions of ceremony.

V. It is planned to have a parade of the Battalion on Memorial Day, May 30, provided enough uniforms and rifles are obtained, and the men are drilled well enough to make a good appearance; for it must be understood that this organization is to be a credit to the fine old town of Port Washington, and that it is no "target company", out for a lark; but on the contrary, has been formed, possibly for serious duty in this hour of our Country's peril; and we hope that, if it becomes necessary, the members who may be called, will reflect credit and glory on the organization and this effort to train them for honorable service.

By Order:
   CLARENCE H. EAGLE,
      *Commanding,*
      *Late Major, N. G. N. Y.*

Within a month of our entry into the war, Clarence H. Eagle, past Major in the New York National Guard, issued Orders No. 1 for Headquarters Home Guard, Port Washington.

Manorhaven's Locust Grove Pavilion and its surrounding land was ideal for the Home Guard encampment. It had previously offered dining, dancing, and bowling to passengers from New York City and the Bronx arriving by excursion steamships.

**Below**: Home Guard application for Charles Wysong, Home Guard Secretary and Treasurer.

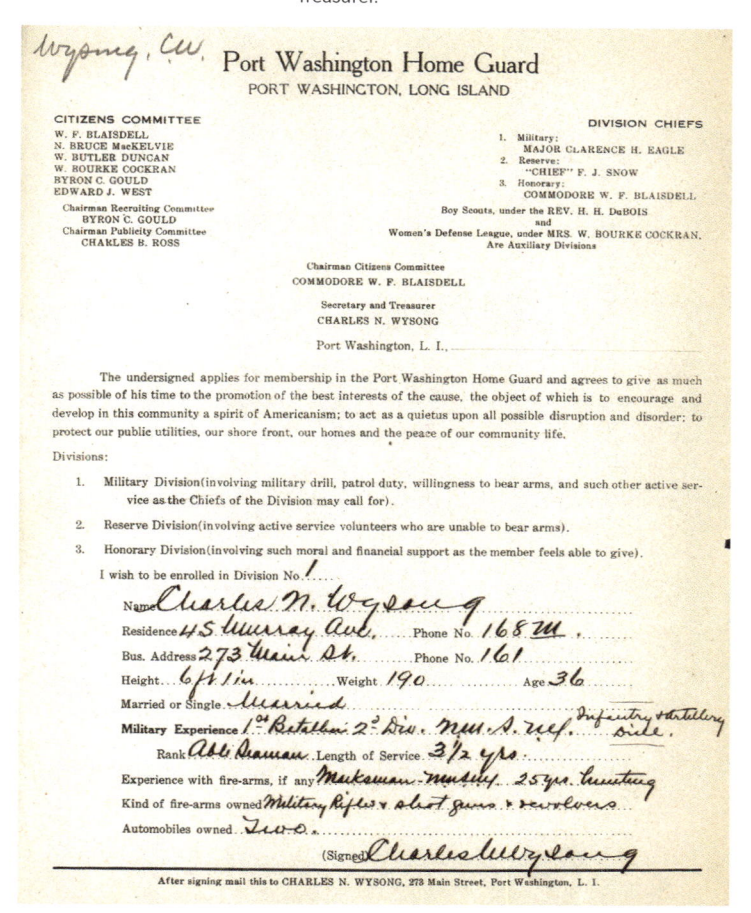

**Top**: Warren Morgan, U.S. Navy Ship's Carpenter, left, and Silas Seaman, U.S. Naval Reserves.

**Left**: Thomas McKee. Young and old alike served their country, some going off to war and some supporting Homefront efforts.

**Below**: Photos of Home Guard at Locust Grove encampment; Home Guard Weekly Time Book; Headquarters, Orders No. 1; All atop listings of Home Guard members' names and addresses.

WWI: The Homefront • Regiment • Cow Neck Peninsula Historical Society

**Left: Top Shelf**
Home Guard Application for H. K. Landis; WWI metal helmet, worn by Martin Cocks*; WWI bayonet sword; Home Guard Application for E.H. Mackey.

**2nd Shelf**
WWI aviator's glasses; Photo of Mineola School aviation students; Daily Mail War Map, large fold-out map**; WWI postcard – "Some Bonnet"; Photo post-WWI, Martin Cocks (center)*; WWI-era eyeglasses and metal case.

**3rd Shelf**
WWI mess kit; Ration heaters, of newspaper and paraffin; Martin Cocks' Honorable Discharge***; WWI bayonet knife, for belt or bayonet; New Testament, inscribed to "Trix"; "The Ship & Gun Drills, U.S. Navy, 1914**; WWI U.S. Army leather holster.

**Bottom Shelf**
WWI canvas gaiters, worn by Martin Cocks*; Home Guard Application for Martin Cocks***; WWI leather gaiters, worn by Martin Cocks*.

\* Donated by Janet Cocks Chudd
\*\* On Loan from Jennifer & Colin Wiggins
\*\*\* Courtesy Local History Center, P.W.P.L.

30  WWI: The Homefront • Regiment • Cow Neck Peninsula Historical Society

**Top:** The new P and G White Laundry Soap, in place of the White Naphtha Soap because naphtha was needed by the military.

**Right:** A sampling of kitchen utensils that were suitable for use at the Locust Grove encampment.

**Right:** Home Guard soldier at Locust Grove.

WWI: The Homefront • Regiment • Cow Neck Peninsula Historical Society

**Top, left:** WWI U.S. Army officer's service coat, 2nd Pioneer Infantry, Adjutant General's Dept.

**Top, right:** WWI Standard U.S. Marine Corps enlisted dress uniform, worn by Martin Cocks.

Martin Cocks enlisted in 1918 and served in France. His Marine Corps unit guarded President Wilson at the Paris Peace Conference. After the war, he was the second mayor of Port Washington North, 1936-1958.

**Uniforms, left to right**

**23rd Regiment Dress Uniform with Shako (cap):** This NYS National Guard Regiment was mustered into service in 1862. The uniform, c. 1910, could have seen WWI service in the Medical Corps; note the caduceus patch, red cross, and green medical arm bands. The three chevrons on the uniform indicate a rank of sergeant. It belonged to Sergeant Harvey H. Allison, Medical Corps, 23rd Regiment, Brooklyn.

**23rd Regiment Short Service Jacket:** For everyday use.

—23rd Regiment uniforms donated by the Estate of Douglas A. Wilke, Grandson of Sgt. Allison

**Squadron "A" Uniform:** Squadron "A" began in 1884 by a group of wealthy NYC gentlemen, later installed as the Cavalry Division of the NYS National Guard. During WWI, 796 members served; 609 becoming commissioned officers. As part of the 105th Machine Gun Battalion, they broke the Hindenburg Line. They were highly decorated, with Medal of Honor recipients. They were housed in the 94th Street Armory.

—From CNPHS Collection

# The Training Camps

In May 1917, a month after our entry into the war, the Army began building training camps for the troops. Camp Upton in Yaphank and Camp Mills in Garden City became two of the three embarkation points for overseas deployment via the LIRR and ferryboats to Brooklyn or Hoboken piers where ships were boarded.

LIRR train ticket, Camp Upton to Penn Station.

## Camp Upton

The Army had three divisions: Regular Army, National Guard, and civilian draftees, who were to be organized as "National Army," with divisions numbered 77 to 91. The 77th was the first to be organized, comprised of men from New York City's melting pot and Long Island, and was housed at Camp Upton.

The roughly 28,000 recruits at Camp Upton learned how to fight with machine guns and bayonets, to throw grenades from the trenches they dug, and to use a tank brought from England for training.

On March 28, 1918, the 77th became the first draftee division to arrive in France and go into the line. By the end of the war, they had distinguished themselves on many fronts.

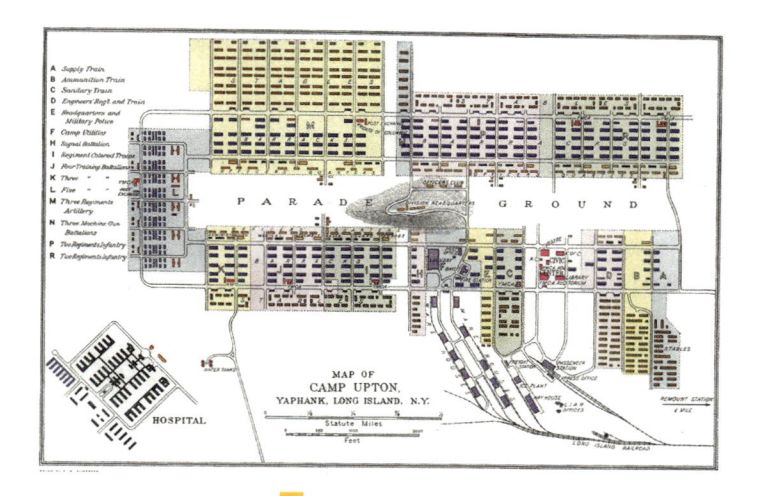

**Top**: Layout map of Camp Upton, Yaphank.
**Below**: Aerial photograph of Camp Upton.

**Below**: African American soldiers training with bayonets.

WWI: The Homefront • Regiment • Cow Neck Peninsula Historical Society  **35**

In 1917, the YWCA engaged architect Katherine C. Budd to design hostess houses for the soldiers' visiting families, complete with dining and rest areas, particularly appreciated by men saying their final goodbyes before shipping out.

**Left:** Parade at Camp Mills.
**Right:** Unit organizational flag of the "Rainbow Division."

## Camp Mills

Camp Mills was comprised of both Regular Army and National Guard. Regular Army troops, numbering 27,000, came from all over the country and our overseas bases. 122,000 National Guard troops, including New York's "Fighting 69th," were mobilized on July 12, 1917.

Douglas MacArthur suggested combining the National Guard units from all across the country "like a rainbow" to avoid anticipated charges of favoritism. He was made the Rainbow Division's first chief of staff, as a colonel. In time, 200,000 troops passed through Camp Mills.

## Mitchel Field Air Force Base

Located on Hempstead Plains next to Camp Mills, Mitchell Field was named in honor of the former NYC mayor, killed while training for air service. Its Hazelhurst fields were two of the largest in the country, where hundreds of aviators were trained. Two Roosevelt fields, named in 1919 for Theodore Roosevelt's son Quentin who was killed in air combat, were utilized to set up wooden buildings and tents to accommodate the great influx of men.

Mitchel Field is now home to Hofstra University, Nassau Community College, Nassau Coliseum, Mitchel Athletic Complex, and the Cradle of Aviation Museum.

**Left:** Aviator goggles.
**Right:** Mineola instructors checking equipment of student about to make a flight.
**Bottom:** Mitchel Field Air Force Base.

WWI: The Homefront • Regiment • Cow Neck Peninsula Historical Society

# From the Collection of Joseph Fay

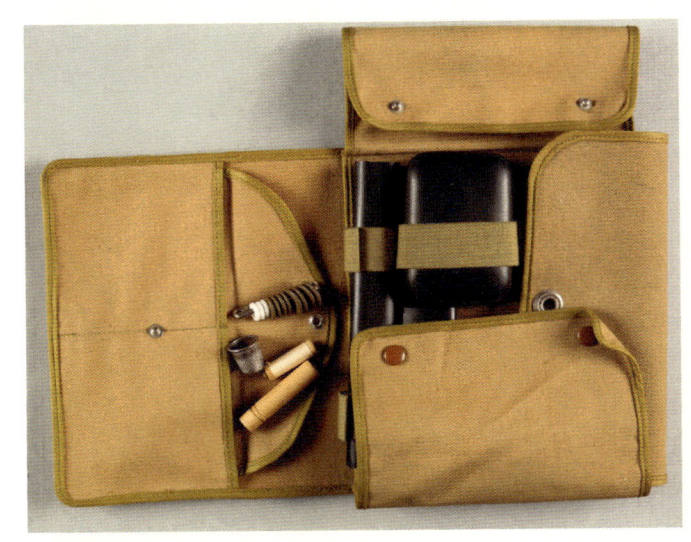

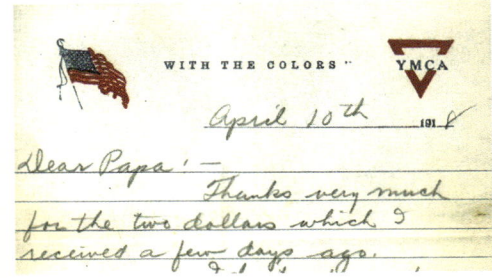

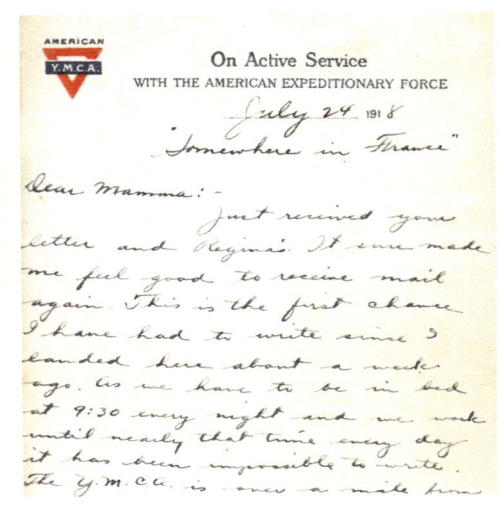

Joseph Fay's personal toiletry kit.

National YMCA stationery, "With the Colors." Letter from Joseph Fay to "Papa," April 10, 1918.

American YMCA stationery, "On Active Service," Letter from Joseph Fay to "Mamma," July 24, 1918.
—On loan from his great-niece, past trustee, Margot Gramer

WWI: The Homefront • Regiment • Cow Neck Peninsula Historical Society

**"On active service with the A. E. F. Nouart (France), Nov. 24th, 1918"**

"...We advanced as far as what was No Man's Land...fell back a little as we were too close to the front line...we were shelled and bombed continuously. One shell hit the pup tent of our sergeant and blew him about 45 feet..."

—**Private Joseph F. Fay, 43rd Balloon Company, Air Service, A.E.F. He was the Port Washington News'** printing plant foreman prior to his service. Letter addressed to his "Dear Papa," reprinted in the Port Washington News, December 20, 1918

**Above:** Tethered kite balloons with observation baskets were used for military surveillance. More stable than round balloons, they could fly at higher altitudes to see things not visible from the ground or ship.

Private Joseph F. Fay at 43rd Balloon School, Camp John A. Wise, Texas, 1918.

WWI: The Homefront • Regiment • Cow Neck Peninsula Historical Society

# Enlistment and Draft

Our country was unprepared for war in 1917.

- APRIL: 120,000 in Army, 80,000 in National Guard, supplies low. Enlistment began. 300,000+ signed up over time.
- MAY: Selective Service Act was enacted for conscription.
- JUNE: Military Census began. 24 million men registered.
- JULY: First draft lottery of 10,500. All drawings done by eligibility category. 2,700,000 were drafted over time.

Training for soldiers and officers was needed. Racism interfered. African Americans, immigrants, and Native Americans were treated poorly and were segregated. They were often assigned to serve in labor units. These groups distinguished themselves despite their harsh treatment.

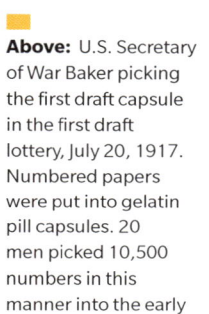

**Above:** U.S. Secretary of War Baker picking the first draft capsule in the first draft lottery, July 20, 1917. Numbered papers were put into gelatin pill capsules. 20 men picked 10,500 numbers in this manner into the early hours of the morning.

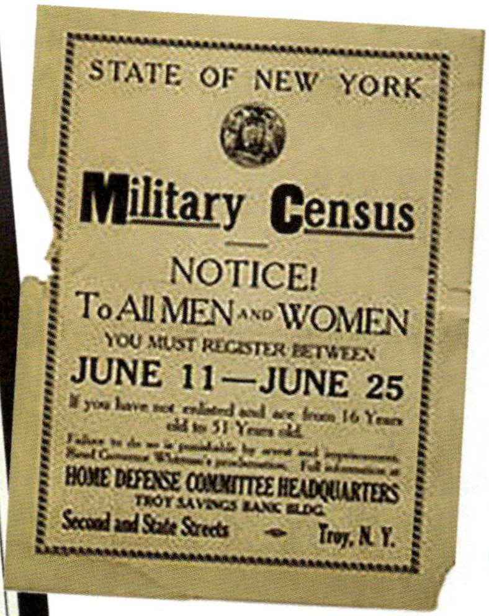

**Top, left:** Port Washington's Mrs. E. LeRoy Finch, recruiting poster model.
**Top, right:** New York State had a military census in 1917 for all men aged 16-51.

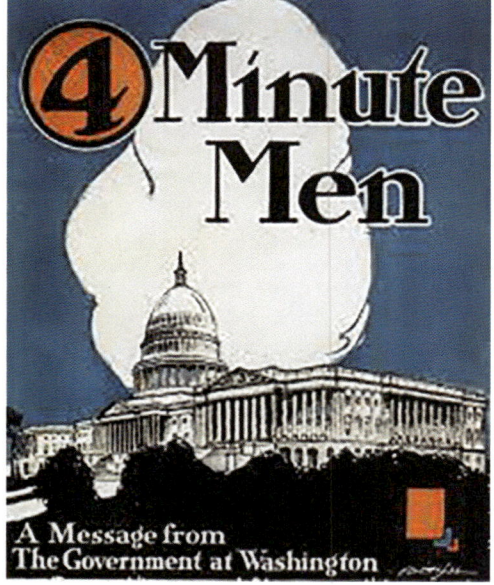

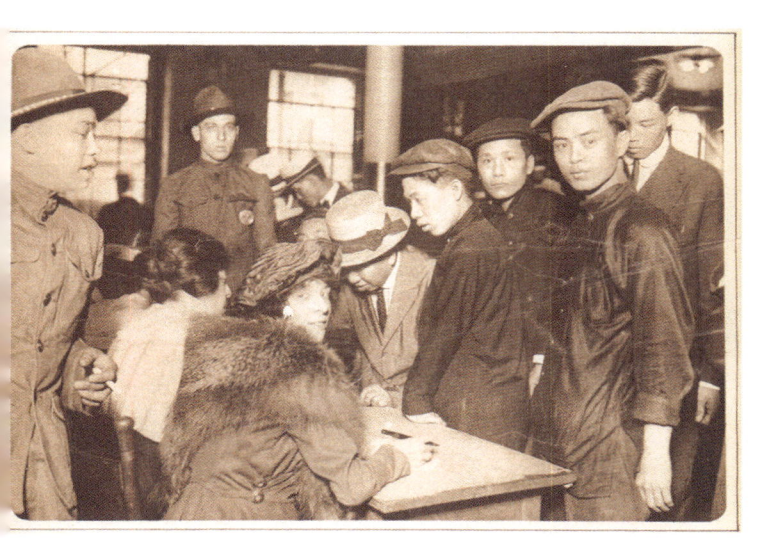

**Left:** Public school teachers registering men for the draft in a Chinese neighborhood.
**Right:** 4 Minute Men recited government-issued propaganda in theaters, religious groups, lodges, unions, to 314 million people, with some hearing the speech many times.

WWI: The Homefront • Regiment • Cow Neck Peninsula Historical Society

Wall Street employees drilled every day at noon atop a skyscraper, a popular New York City drilling site.

Patriotic Fervor Sweeps Eastern Cities

**Left:** Men who drilled on Governor's Island, not yet issued real guns; parading here in City Hall Park with wooden ones.

**Far left:** The President ordered Navy to recruit 26,000 more men immediately.
**Left:** Recruiting stations were set up in novel venues like this mock battleship to attract the men.

Wooden model of a battleship in Union Square, New York City, used as a recruiting station for the United States Navy.

42  WWI: The Homefront • Regiment • Cow Neck Peninsula Historical Society

*July 20, 1917*

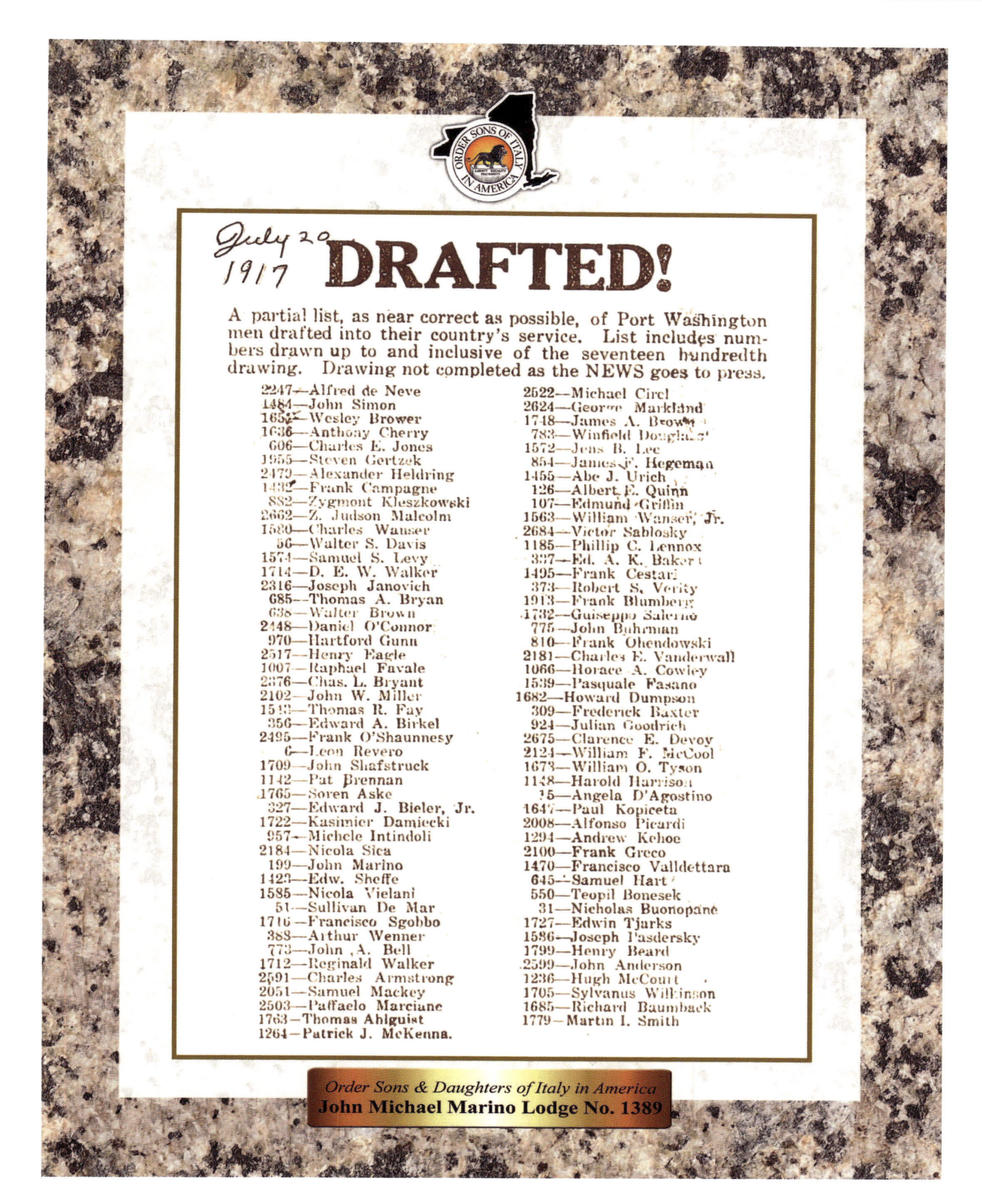

# DRAFTED!

A partial list, as near correct as possible, of Port Washington men drafted into their country's service. List includes numbers drawn up to and inclusive of the seventeen hundredth drawing. Drawing not completed as the NEWS goes to press.

2247—Alfred de Neve
1484—John Simon
1652—Wesley Brower
1636—Anthony Cherry
606—Charles E. Jones
1955—Steven Gertzek
2479—Alexander Heldring
1432—Frank Campagne
882—Zygmont Kleszkowski
2662—Z. Judson Malcolm
1580—Charles Wanser
56—Walter S. Davis
1574—Samuel S. Levy
1714—D. E. W. Walker
2316—Joseph Janovich
685—Thomas A. Bryan
638—Walter Brown
2448—Daniel O'Connor
970—Hartford Gunn
2517—Henry Eagle
1007—Raphael Favale
2376—Chas. L. Bryant
2102—John W. Miller
1512—Thomas R. Fay
356—Edward A. Birkel
2495—Frank O'Shaunnesy
6—Leon Revero
1709—John Shafstruck
1142—Pat Brennan
1765—Soren Aske
327—Edward J. Bieler, Jr.
1722—Kasimier Damiecki
957—Michele Intindoli
2184—Nicola Sica
199—John Marino
1423—Edw. Sheffe
1585—Nicola Vielani
51—Sullivan De Mar
1716—Francisco Sgobbo
388—Arthur Wenner
773—John A. Bell
1712—Reginald Walker
2591—Charles Armstrong
2051—Samuel Mackey
2503—Paffaelo Marciane
1763—Thomas Ahlquist
1264—Patrick J. McKenna.

2522—Michael Circl
2624—George Markland
1748—James A. Brown
783—Winfield Douglas
1572—Jens B. Lee
854—James F. Hegeman
1455—Abe J. Urich
126—Albert E. Quinn
107—Edmund Griffin
1563—William Wanser, Jr.
2684—Victor Sablosky
1185—Phillip C. Lennox
337—Ed. A. K. Baker
1495—Frank Cestari
373—Robert S. Verity
1913—Frank Blumberg
1732—Guiseppo Salerno
775—John Buhrman
810—Frank Ohendowski
2181—Charles E. Vanderwall
1066—Horace A. Cowley
1539—Pasquale Fasano
1682—Howard Dumpson
309—Frederick Baxter
924—Julian Goodrich
2675—Clarence E. Devoy
2124—William F. McCool
1673—William O. Tyson
1138—Harold Harrison
15—Angela D'Agostino
1647—Paul Kopiceta
2008—Alfonso Picardi
1294—Andrew Kehoe
2100—Frank Greco
1470—Francisco Valldettara
645—Samuel Hart
550—Teopil Bonesek
31—Nicholas Buonopane
1727—Edwin Tjarks
1586—Joseph Pasdersky
1799—Henry Beard
2599—John Anderson
1236—Hugh McCourt
1705—Sylvanus Wilkinson
1685—Richard Baumback
1779—Martin I. Smith

*Order Sons & Daughters of Italy in America*
**John Michael Marino Lodge No. 1389**

# Correspondence from France

The following is a letter that Mr. and Mrs. James Poole of Prospect Avenue received from their son Clyde, who enlisted in the Motor Transport Corps in Columbus, Ohio, where he has for some time been employed. He was married to Miss Hilda Wood, a former resident of Port Washington, a few days after his enlistment.

*No. 688 Motor Transport Co.*
*Nov. 25th, 1918*

*My dear Mother and Father:*
*I have not received a letter from you in several weeks but am looking for one every day. Paris is a beautiful and wonderful city. Yesterday I went to church in the morning and in the afternoon I went to see some of the interesting parts of the city. I went to see Napoleon's Tomb for one thing and the Eiffel Tower for another, and they are only two of a number of things I saw. I could write all day and still not tell you all I saw and never could I describe it. It certainly was beautiful.*

*You will notice that my company's name and number have been changed by the above The whole 812th Motor Car Co. has changed to the 688th Motor Transport Company. It seems impossible to me that next Thursday is Thanksgiving and a month from today Christmas, and that I won't be home for either. Never mind, no matter when I arrive it certainly will be a great holiday for me. I only wish that Hilda was here with me to see some of the wonderful things I have seen since I have been here.*

*I have also seen some of the great damage done when they were fighting so near Paris and also some of the damage done by air raids. I drove a Cadillac touring car from Bordeaux to Paris and it was a very pretty trip. I was very glad to get those clippings from the Port Washington News especially the local items. I only wish that I could have got some German trophies to have sent home and to keep in my own home when I return. Maybe I will have the chance before I return. Hoping this will find you and father in the best of health, I remain,*

*Your loving son,*
*CLYDE*

— **Port Washington News, 27th December, 1918**

Thomas Goodwin of Adams Street received the following letter from his son, Fred, who was in the 12th Co., 4th Mechanics Regiment, Aviation Service. Fred, sharing a brief account of his trip overseas, finally got this letter past the censor.

*On Active Service*
*British Expeditionary Force*
*November 23, 1918*

*Dear Dad,*
*Today is Father's Day so I thought you would look for a letter from me. Well, Dad, did you receive my last letter? If you did, don't forget to answer it: this is a chance. When we left New York I knew that I was in the game. We left next morning after seeing you and Mother; three days after we reached "H" we started on our trip across. We got three "Subs" on the way over. Not bad, eh?*

*When we landed at "L" England, it was about 11 in the morning, so we had a good look at. We left there for a southern port, "S. H.," and it took a day to get there. Then we waited for a dark night to cross to France to a northern port "La H.," where they had a raid the night before without anyone being killed. We could hear the big guns at the front all night and left there three days after and went to "P." and from there to this place, it was quite a trip.*

*Last night "Dick" Smith, "Art" Fay, Tom Poulson and myself ran together in the Y.M.C.A. "Dick" has been here for two months, "Art" about a month, and I was sure glad to see them.*

*Well, it is late, Dad. So I will close with love to all and wish you a Merry Christmas and a Happy New Year.*

*From your son,*
*Fred*

*Address: Fred Goodwin, 12 th Co., 4th Mech. Regt. A.S.S.A.I., Co/o P.O. 724, American Expeditionary Force.*

(We judge that "H" would stand for Hoboken. "L" for London. "S.H." and "P" for Paris. It would appear that letters are still undergoing rigid inspection. This letter bears the O.K. of young Mr. Goodwin's commanding officer. Captain F. Connell)

—**Port Washington News, December 27th, 1918**

New York City's 69th Infantry saying goodbye to their sweethearts at L.I.R.R. in 1917 after a brief training at Camp Mills.

**History of the Seventy-Seventh Division– August 25th, 1917 – November 11th, 1918**, published in 1919, was designed and written in the field in France by the officers and men of the Division – quite an achievement. This was John Nicolas Huwer's book, great-uncle of CNPHS Past President, Fred Blumlein. John Huwer trained with Camp Upton's 77th Division and shipped out to France as a wagoner, caring for and driving mule teams pulling ammunition and supplies.

The 77th Division was the first National Army Division in Europe and the first responsible for an active sector, the Argonne. Comprised of men of all races and creeds from New York City, newly arrived immigrants and long time residents, this motley crew became known as the Liberty Division.

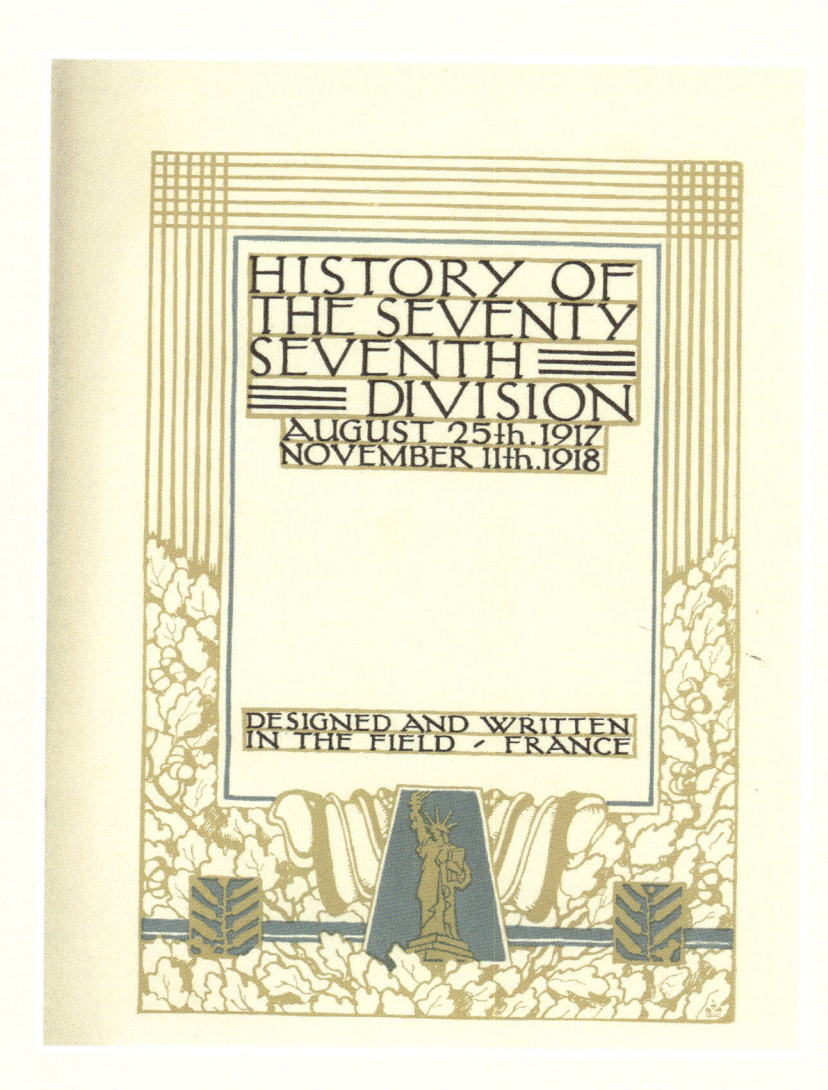

**NEW YORK'S OWN**

A clerk removed his well-worn hat,
From the rack on the office hall;
An artist laid his brushes by,
And a mason left his maul;
The iceman quit his clanking tongs,
And the mailman ceased his rounds;
While a millionaire's son jacked up his car,
And locked his country grounds.

So Paddy Ryan and Percival Nail
Left side by side for the tough travail;
In every alley-way and street,
The terrible tread of marching feet
Forewarned the Hun, with ominous ring,
That "New York's Own" were marshalling
Their rainbow hosts for battle-tasks.
And when the wide world idly asks,
"Where are the men who did not fail?"
They're Paddy Ryan and Percival Nail!

—Poem reprinted from the book

48  WWI: The Homefront • Farmerettes • Cow Neck Peninsula Historical Society

# Farmerettes

"The Canning Kitchen has been most busy lately. They now have on hand 1,141 quarts of vegetables and fruit and from three to four hundred glasses of jelly. These are for the soldiers I believe. The kitchen has been quoted as the second most efficient kitchen on Long Island, for the size of its enterprise."

—Port Washington News, October 5, 1917

# Farmerettes of Long Island

"The farmer is pleased with the work of the land army – he declared that the farm has never paid so well as it has since the women came into his employ."

– The National League for Woman's Service

Food was needed for local consumption, to allow basic resources like wheat and meat to be sent overseas to feed both soldiers and starving civilians. Farmerettes were in great demand all over the country to replace the men, despite initial resistance. Closer to home, "Long Island inhabitants were among the first to welcome the girl with the hoe."

—Port Washington News, 9/13/1918

50   WWI: The Homefront • Farmerettes • Cow Neck Peninsula Historical Society

Society woman Ruth Litt of Patchogue plowing her 135-acre farm where she hired an all-female crew. Locally, farmerettes were hired in Sands Point at the estates of Isaac and Daniel Guggenheim and on Barkers Point on the property of Mary Nostrand.

Farmingdale Agricultural College offered a course to farmerettes, most of whom were novices. New barracks were built due to demand. In 1917, over 170 acres were planted; they had 10 milk cows, 17 hogs, and a poultry plant.

### The Farmerette Shoe
*For War Gardeners*

UNCLE SAM is going to harvest a bumper crop this season and in his aid he has enlisted thousands of young women throughout the country.

Correct clothing for the farmerette will be found at Loeser's in good variety, including the NEW FARMERETTE SHOE, which, we are informed, cannot be found generally.

These Shoes were especially designed for young women who will do farm work and other war service that requires sturdy, comfortable footwear. Made of tan colored chrome side leather, soft and mellow, yet serviceable. Unlined. Goodyear welted and stitched soles of a chrome tannage, known generally as an elk sole. Square low heels. Lace style to toe.

A very flexible and comfortable Shoe : **$5.50** a pair.

WWI: The Homefront • Farmerettes • Cow Neck Peninsula Historical Society

100 acres in Port Washington were offered to residents for cultivation. Those north of Main Street got plots at Mr. Cockran's to grow corn. Those on the south side went to the Copp property or Port Washington Estates to grow beans and cabbage. Women from the community pledged 48 hours per week, and men and children were encouraged to work on Saturdays or in the evenings.

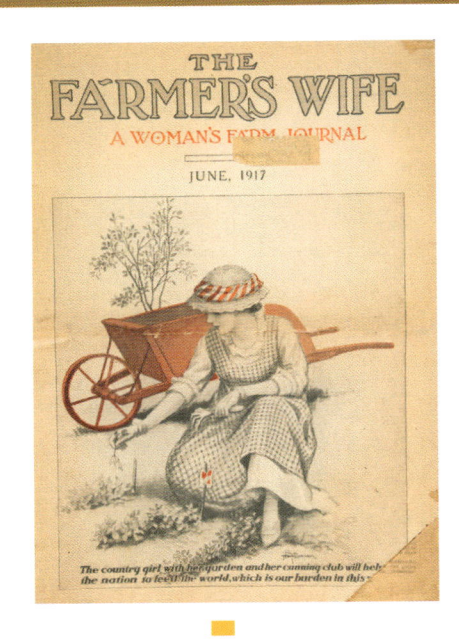

**Bottom:** Young farmerettes heading into the fields for a good day's work.

*The Farmer's Wife— A Woman's Farm Journal,* June 1917.

"Owing to the continued demand for farm workers, 8 girls are wanted at once for the Port Washington Land Army…"

(Brooklyn Daily Eagle, 8/29/1918)

**Above:** The #12 Trolley connecting Port Washington to Mineola via Roslyn. An ad appears on the cowcatcher in front of the trolley, this one for a "Bairn Dance."

## Farmerettes on the Move

Some farmerettes took a 28¢ trolley ride from Port Washington to work in Mineola. It was 25 minutes to the Roslyn Clock Tower, where they waited for the northbound trolley to pass before continuing. The dark green trolleys had light green interiors and rattan seats.

WWI: The Homefront • Farmerettes • Cow Neck Peninsula Historical Society

Trolleys were instrumental in moving the farmerettes. 100 acres of land between Farmingdale and Huntington were set up for farming specifically along the trolley line. The trolley also provided a means of entertainment for the young women. Roslyn farmerettes often took the trolley to Port Washington for an evening out. Sands Point farmerettes were too far away to use the trolley so Manhasset Bay Yacht Club started a fund drive to buy them a car.

The food grown by the farmerettes was utilized locally and also further afield. Vegetables from Roslyn supplied the grand hotels of the city: the Waldorf Astoria, the Plaza, the Ritz-Carlton, and the St. Regis.

**Above:** Illustration for Kurz Oil calendar by Bill Galloway. Text reads: "Victoria Hotel built by Walter & Richard Mullon, (1905), at corner of Haven & Main Sts. Troll[e]y cars between Port- Washington & Mineola, (1908- 1920), carried 'farmerettes' in World War I."

**Top:** The trolley passing the Clock Tower in the Village of Roslyn.

**Bottom:** Farmerettes lucky to have a car en route to work.

54 WWI: The Homefront • Farmerettes • Cow Neck Peninsula Historical Society

# The Canning Special

In response to the call to preserve foods, the L.I.R.R. set up instructional canning trains that traversed the Island. A number of towns also established community canning kitchens. Port Washington set up a very successful one in the Bayles Building at the corner of Main Street and Shore Road.

WWI: The Homefront • Farmerettes • Cow Neck Peninsula Historical Society

## FRIDAY ITINERARY OF THE CANNING SPECIAL

Auburndale ........ from 9:30 a.m. to 10:30 a.m.
Great Neck ......... from 10:45 a.m. to 11:45 a.m.
Pt. Washington .. from 12:00 a.m. to 1:00 p.m.
Jamaica ............... from 2:30 p.m. to 3:30 p.m.
Cedarhurst ........ from 4:00 p.m. to 5:00 p.m.

Three days a week, a demonstrator canned produce that women would bring in. It was sent to the soldiers at the front or sold to keep the program going. On other days, women could can their own produce, including cherries, carrots, asparagus, peas, spinach, strawberry juice, and rhubarb jam. Some even preserved chicken meat for chicken pie or soup in the winter.

**Top:** L.I.R.R. freight and passenger cars were custom fit as a canning kitchen, a lecture coach, a baggage car to hold all the canning supplies, and a business car for the women in charge.

**Bottom:** New York society women, in a L.I.R.R. "Canning Special" train, spread both alarm at the food shortage and information and demonstrations on canning. They came to Port Washington on May 24, 1917.

"Certainly will look after your babies while you hear the lecture." Mrs. William K. Vanderbilt appointed herself as watcher of any children, so mothers could go aboard.

**Above:** "Society Women in freight cars teach canning to housewives of Long Island, N.Y. 1917."

**Left:** The Canning Special "Victory Special Food Demonstration Car," 1917.

WWI: The Homefront • Farmerettes • Cow Neck Peninsula Historical Society

# Sow the Seeds of Victory!

During WWI, European farms turned into battlefields. Farmers became soldiers. America was needed to help feed millions of starving people long before we entered the war.

Americans rationed their meat, wheat, sugar, and fat. We ate less and wasted less. We grew more and grew it locally, saving on transportation resources.

58  WWI: The Homefront • Farmerettes • Cow Neck Peninsula Historical Society

New farming and gardening movements emerged, and food preservation techniques were taught. Reinforcing posters, slogans, and articles appeared everywhere.

Increased food exports contributed to our victory in the war.

## Seed Produces Food

Europe had a shortage of food and a shortage of seed. America filled the need, becoming the leading supplier of seed. Patriotic catalog covers were designed to encourage production.

## Women's Land Army

The farmerettes were initially controversial – *"A woman's place is in the home."* But this woman-organized group put 20,000 farming women in 25 states from 1917-1919, to replace the men gone to war.

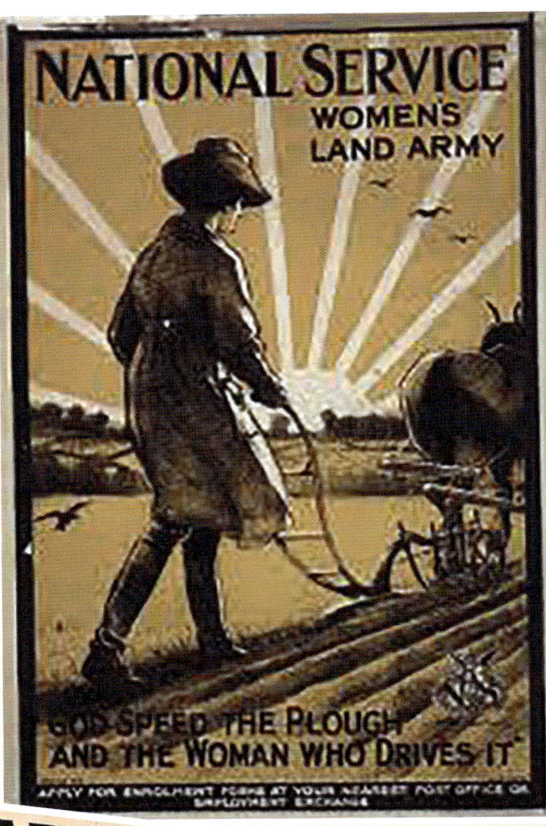

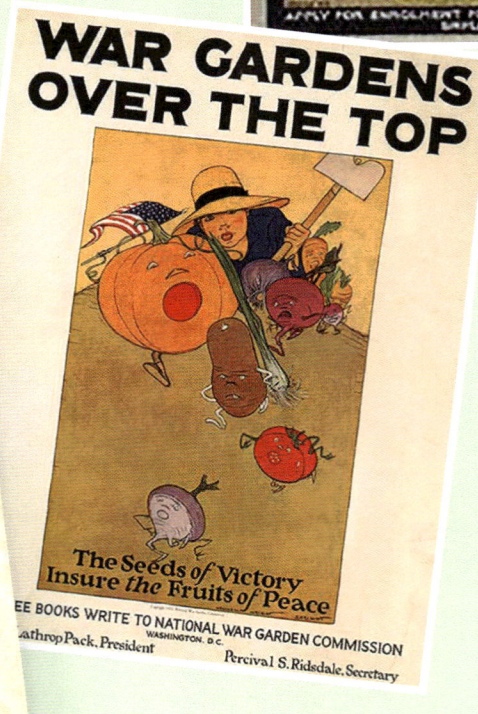

## National War Garden Commission

This group fostered food production and gave instruction, including on the use of fertilizer. Our community gardened passionately and successfully but would not use fertilizer.

60  WWI: The Homefront • Farmerettes • Cow Neck Peninsula Historical Society

### Suffragist Farmers

Many suffragists chose to put their fight for suffrage aside to fully support the war effort, like these gardeners. More militant suffrage groups split off and remained resolute. A combination of both led to their success.

### US School Garden Army

This war effort was a great success: By 1919, 2.5 million children were involved, producing $48 million worth of food – in 1919 dollars.

Children received manuals that taught:
- To keep tools clean just like a soldier.
- How to avoid sprains when weeding.
- Reminders not to step on the seedlings.

The school garden movement had successful prototypes to pave the way prior to the war. The above photo of DeWitt Clinton Park, located in NYC's Hell's Kitchen, had 360 plots on ¾ of an acre.

WWI: The Homefront • Farmerettes • Cow Neck Peninsula Historical Society

## Food will win the War

Britain had only 3-4 weeks of food left by Spring 1917 despite our aid. Then we entered the war and needed to feed our own soldiers. Greater food management was needed.

The U.S. Food Administration was born with future president Herbert Hoover at the helm. He wanted no pay, to better ask for sacrifice. Detractors called his program "Hooverizing" and him the "food dictator," but he made the difference.

Hang this where you will see it every day.

**United States Food Administration**

**REMEMBER THE DAYS**

SUNDAY .....—One meal Wheatless; one meal Meatless.
MONDAY ....—All meals Wheatless; one meal Meatless.
TUESDAY ....—All meals Meatless; one meal Wheatless.
WEDNESDAY—All meals Wheatless; one meal Meatless.
THURSDAY ..—One meal Wheatless; one meal Meatless.
FRIDAY ......—One meal Wheatless; one meal Meatless.
SATURDAY ..—All meals Porkless; one meal Wheatless; one meal Meatless.

Keep Good Food Out of Your Garbage Pail and Kitchen Sink
Don't Feed High-Priced Human Food to Hogs or Chickens

**WASTE NO FOOD!**

HOUSEHOLD WASTE ABOUT 700 MILLION DOLLARS

HOOVER CARD FOR WHO'EVER WANTS IT

Although the days be wheatless,
And meatless, sweetless, too,
They never can be treatless
While I can think of you.

Housewives signed his pledge for food conservation. A Hoover Helper's Uniform or Hoover Apron was designed for both instructors and housewives. This reversible garment had removable cuffs and collar to save on laundering. A pattern was 10¢.

We saw meatless Tuesdays and wheatless Wednesdays. We used less fat and sugar and had less waste. More produce was grown and used locally. We kept hens in the backyard, and President Wilson grazed sheep on the White House lawns.

*The Ladies' Home Journal for September, 1917*  27

# THE WOMAN AND THE WAR

A War Service Bringing the American Woman in Close Touch With Her Government

Edited by
**DUDLEY HARMON**
At THE LADIES' HOME JOURNAL'S Washington Bureau: Woodward Building, Washington, D.C.

## Questions That Women Ask Mr. Hoover

### Answered Here So That Every Woman in America May Know What She Can Do to Help the Food Administration

SO MANY questions have come to the Food Administration from women that the present opportunity is taken to present the answers to those that have arisen most frequently and seem most generally puzzling or misunderstood. For example:

### Don't Stop Eating All White Bread

*Is it not true that a steady diet of corn meal or whole wheat or bran is not entirely good for us?*

MANY people find it so from experience, but it is not necessary to stop entirely eating bread made from white flour. For instance, a good plan is to eat white bread at one meal; corn bread the next, whole-wheat bread the next, and then revert to white bread. At no time has a total abstinence from white bread been recommended, merely its wise conservation.

### Why Should We Eat More Potatoes?

*Just what is your idea in urging a greater consumption of potatoes?*

EVERY extra potato eaten this year will be a direct contribution to the amount of food available for shipment to Europe. It is by reducing our consumption of such foods as, particularly, wheat, beef, pork, etc., which can readily be shipped to Europe, while potatoes cannot, that we are going to be able to feed our Allies in their time of great need. Increase in our potato consumption will more or less automatically bring about less use of other foods. Besides, you will, by greater potato consumption, help the farmer.

### Four-O'Clock Teas

*You urge the stopping of four-o'clock teas; why? Is it due to a wish to conserve tea?*

NO; IT is not on account of the tea, but of what is served, by custom, with it—cakes, cookies, wheat-bread sandwiches. All these involve the use of wheat flour and are not essentially foods. Therefore eliminating them will work no hardship and the flour in them will be released for use where it is essential.

### Why Lamb Should Not be Eaten

*Am I right in assuming that you wish us to stop eating very young lamb? Why?*

YES, and because it is vitally necessary for that lamb to become a mature sheep and thus produce more wool for clothing.

### The Eating of Sugar

*You ask us to stop consuming sugar; doesn't the body demand it?*

IT CERTAINLY does, and the Food Administration has never urged people to "stop consuming sugar." It has, however, urged people to stop wasting it. Statistics show that the average American consumes three times as much sugar as any one of our Allies. All that is urged is that some of this sugar that obviously is consumed for the sweet tooth's, and not the body's, sake be not thus consumed. Moreover, the housewife, as well as the rest of the family, will find that honey, sirups and molasses are excellent substitutes for sugar in sweetening cakes and candies.

### Why Our Wheat Must Go Abroad

*Why must so much of our wheat go abroad? Why can't our Allies use corn?*

BECAUSE they do not know corn as we do. They wouldn't know what to do with it, and this is no time to ask fighting men to try new things. They do know wheat; it is literally Europe's staff of life, and that is why we who know corn must eat as much corn as possible and let our Allies have our wheat. Besides which, Europe is now mixing its wheat flour all the barley and oats that the peoples can stand.

### Why Should We Save Coal?

*What relation has the saving of coal to the food problem?*

COAL comes from a distance. It must be brought to you by the railroads. The railroads are going to have their hands full to move the troops, and to get supplies to the camps and food to the seaboard. You will distinctly help by saving coal and thus minimizing its transportation.

### An Easy Way to Save Flour

*How can I, in one way, save white flour in my small household?*

IN THE way you serve bread. Cut it at the table, slice by slice, as it is wanted. Save the uneaten ends of the loaf, convert into crumbs and use them in puddings, breakfast cakes and muffins.

### Husbands Must Help

*I am willing enough to save as I am urged to do, but often my husband complains. What shall I do?*

THE man who complains at the result of his wife's efforts to conserve food is doing her an inexcusable injury. He should never hesitate to coöperate in her wise conservation plans. Every man should join the Food Administration.

### Why No Second Helpings

*You have urged against second helpings at table; why?*

BECAUSE overly generous second helpings are too often not consumed and what is left on the individual plate is generally wasted. A generous single helping is more desirable.

### Meatless Days

*Is it true that you approve meatless days?*

YES, as a simple system of domestic meat conservation. Eat more fish and less meat generally. Meat for breakfast is unnecessary; eggs and cereals are good substitutes for it.

### When to Use Butter

*How can we do without butter, as we are asked?*

YOU are not asked to do without butter; you are asked to conserve butter. Use all that is necessary on the table. Children particularly need it. But in cooking use other fats, as drippings, vegetable oils and butter substitutes.

---

### HOW YOU WILL KNOW HER

HERE are the official badge and uniform of members of the Food Administration of the United States. Any woman who signs the Hoover pledge is entitled to wear them. The uniform is of blue chambray, with pointed collar and cuffs of white piqué and cap of white lawn. Its cost, made at home, will be from one dollar to one dollar and twenty-five cents. All the pieces can be easily laundered, as they open out flat. The cap is fastened by snaps. The cuffs are detachable. The dress has a double front; if one panel becomes soiled the other may be brought outside. It is fastened by two straps, either of which may be passed through a slit and the ends buttoned at the back. There are two pockets on the skirt. The collar, cap and cuffs, white; the insignia are embroidered in red, white and blue, surrounded by yellow wheat. Patterns for the Hoover Helper's Uniform may be obtained by members of the Food Administration by sending ten cents to the Food Administrator, at Washington, D.C.

---

### Other Ways to Save Wheat

*Which foods can I best reduce the use of in my home to save white flour? How about wheatless meals?*

CAKE and pastry. We eat much more cake and pastry than is good for us and it will be easy to reduce the amount. If you will eat even white bread with discretion and cut out from fifty to seventy-five per cent of your cake and pastry, it will help immensely. Three wheatless meals a week would mean one wheatless day.

### Use Milk a-Plenty

*We should use milk a-plenty, should we not?*

DECIDEDLY yes. Especially for children. Let them drink all the milk you can afford to buy and that they relish. Use buttermilk and sour milk, too, the latter in cooking and the making of cottage cheese. This latter might well appear on the luncheon table much oftener than it does.

### Eating Less Pork

*We are asked to cut down our consumption of pork; why?*

BECAUSE pork products have a high proportion of fats, which are desperately needed abroad by our Allies, whose own supplies of fats are diminishing; besides which, pork products are readily shipped abroad.

### Seeing the Farmer Through

*You ask us to help the farmer with his potatoes; how do you mean?*

THE farmer planted more potatoes this year than ever before and is now raising a bumper crop, largely because it was urged upon him as a patriotic duty. If those of us who shouted to the farmer to save us by raising more potatoes fail to take them off his hands he will have a just cause for grievance. Furthermore, the farmer has a good memory and, should he face a financial loss on his potato growing this year through a failure of the public to eat what six months ago we begged him to raise, he will be slow to respond in the future to any appeal telling him what to raise.

### The Waste in Restaurants

*How about the waste in hotels and restaurants? Is anything being done about it?*

THERE is; the hotels and restaurants are falling into line with the finest kind of coöperation. A hotel can help their proprietors by not ordering those things that should be conserved. A hotel won't long supply what its guests do not demand.

### Where Can a Woman Learn?

*Where can I intelligently learn your ideas of food conservation?*

DURING the early summer thousands of teachers received special instruction in the summer schools in the gospel of saving food in war time. There is now a host of women ready to give food instruction to women wherever they can be assembled, whether in crossroads schoolhouse, town hall or city meeting place. If you don't know what arrangements, if any, have been made in your community for lessons and demonstrations in the better use of food, here are the things you can do and should do:

(1) Get into touch with the Food Administration's representative in your community.
(2) Make inquiry of a domestic science or other school-teacher or the school authorities.
(3) Get in touch with the woman agent in your county of the State College of Agriculture; or, if there is no county agent, write to the Extension Division of your State College of Agriculture and see if the services of a county agent or some other competent person can be secured to come to your community and organize a class in foods. If this is not practicable,
(4) Ask the Extension Division of your State College of Agriculture how you can take a correspondence course in foods and home management, and thus go to school in your own home.
(5) Ask the pastor of your church, for the churches are advancing the cause of food conservation in every community.

Some of the classes—most, in fact—will be free to all women willing to join them. To other classes small fees will be charged. Some women naturally will find the opportunity for instruction in food saving brought directly to them. Other women, of course, will have to seek their opportunity.

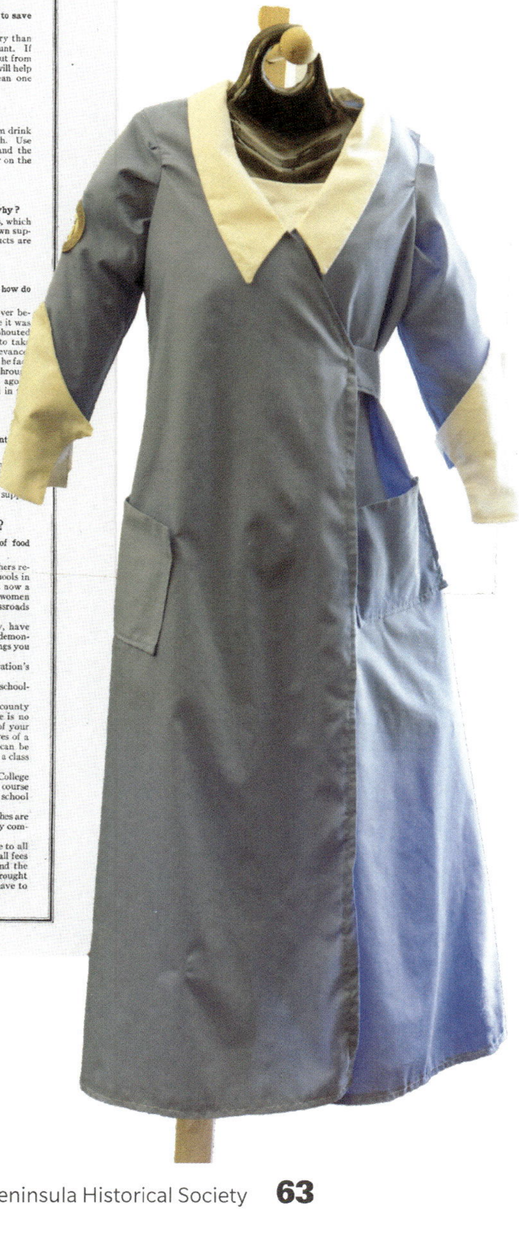

---

**WWI: The Homefront • Farmerettes • Cow Neck Peninsula Historical Society**  **63**

**Right:** "The Delineator for September 1918," ad for Victory Bread depicting woman in Hoover apron.

**Bottom:** "The Ladies Home Journal for September, 1918 'A Whole Meal Canned in One Jar.'"

"One of the most energetic of the ladies… decided that it was far cheaper to keep her hens in glass jars, after they had finished laying, than to feed them all winter, so that one may have a chicken pie or a nice pot of soup in the cold weather. So on Thursday at the Canning Kitchen three of her older hens were nicely potted, some of the fowl for meat and some for delicious soup."

—Port Washington News, June 15th, 1917

## Ration Posters

The poster was the most widely used means of mass communication during the WWI era. The government needed to reach all citizens – rural, urban, immigrants in other languages, and with images for the illiterate. Posters were also able to provide constant reinforcement.

Food ration posters appealed to one's patriotic duty and volunteerism. Other types of posters, for example, those about enlistment, more often utilized propaganda, coercion, and shame.

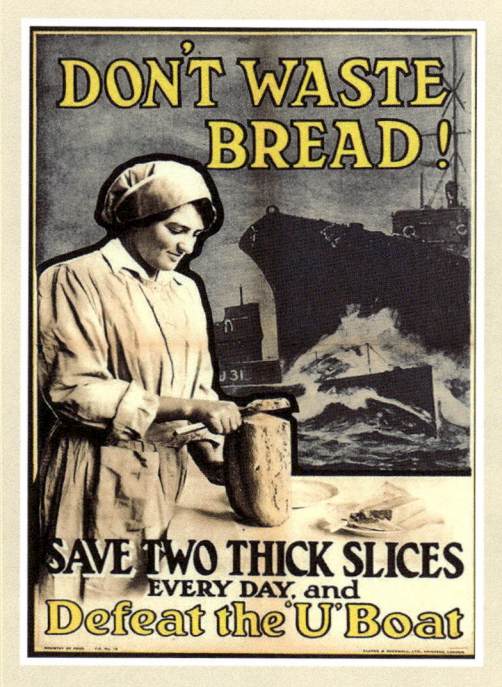

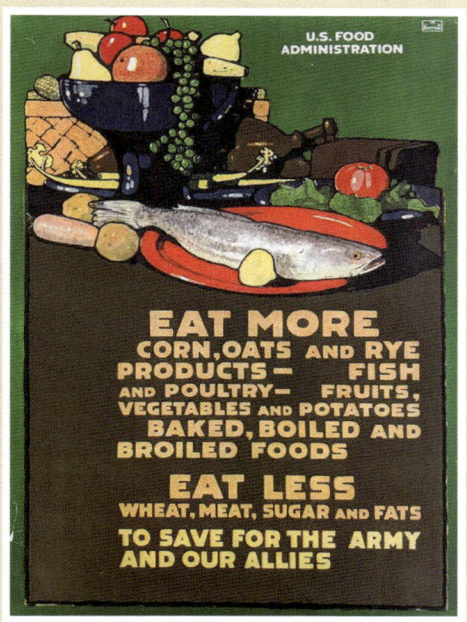

WWI: The Homefront • Farmerettes • Cow Neck Peninsula Historical Society

WWI: The Homefront • Regiment • Cow Neck Peninsula Historical Society

# The War Effort

"The Boy Scouts have done a useful work, and the readiness and efficiency with which they did it, particularly during the war period, justifies our earnest hope that their usefulness may be continued and enhanced in the future."

—President Warren G. Harding, March 17, 1921

# 300,000 Boy Heroes

The Boy Scouts of America was the nation's largest uniformed organization when we entered the war, larger than ¾ of the combined Armed Forces.

A presidential citation was issued for their achievements, which included:
- Emergency coast patrol and message runners with their knowledge of signal flags and Morse Code – a governmental request.
- Work with the Red Cross to aid sick and wounded soldiers with their first aid and life-saving training.
- "Every scout to feed a soldier" – They actually fed 2-3 soldiers each by gardening.
- Sold ½ billion dollars of Liberty Loan Bonds / War Savings Stamps.
- Collected 100 carloads of peach pits for carbon extraction.

**Below, top:** Boy Scouts encouraging people in New York City to buy Liberty Bonds.
**Below, bottom:** Boy Scouts charging down Fifth Avenue in "Wake Up, America!" parade in New York City, April 19, 1917, two weeks after our war entry. 60,000 people attended.

WWI: The Homefront • Regiment • Cow Neck Peninsula Historical Society

**Top**: A black walnut grove. Scouts planted three new trees for each one harvested. (Photo: Creative Commons)

**Inset:** William Guggenheim's home, 150-acre Waterside Farm in Sands Point, now Harriman Estates. (Photo: P.W.P.L Local History Center)

**Left**: Posters, books and word of mouth encouraged boys to become actively involved with Scouting and the war effort.

Black walnut wood was strong enough to use for propellers and gun stocks. It was hard to find because German agents had already scoured Long Island. But the largest stash was on William Guggenheim's Sands Point property, where he had roughly 200 trees. The Boy Scouts, tasked with finding these trees, located 20,000 board feet of wood in their search.

WWI: The Homefront • Regiment • Cow Neck Peninsula Historical Society    **69**

# Liberty Loan Bonds

"You Buy A Liberty Bond. Lest I perish. Get Behind The Government."

—Charles R. Macaulay, Poster for the U.S. Food Administration for the Liberty Loan of 1917

**Right**: Window placard for a subscriber of the WWI Victory Liberty Loan.

**Middle**: WWI Woman's Liberty Loan Committee armband with two slits for band.
—Donated by Susan Murphy

**Far, right**: 1918 WWI War Service Medal for Boy Scouts presented by U.S. Treasury Dept. for service in Liberty Loan Campaign.
—Donated by Scoutmaster Chris Simone, Plandome Troop 71

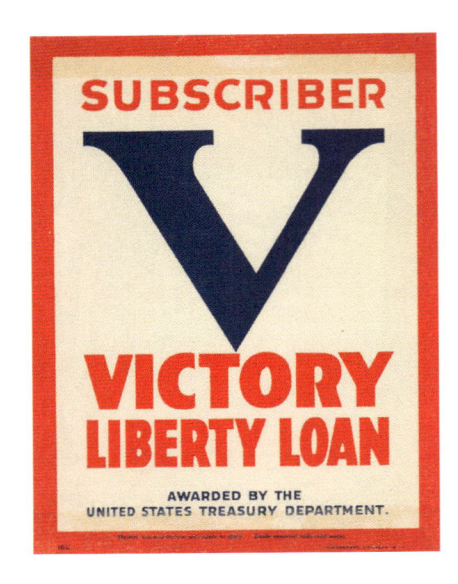

70 WWI: The Homefront • Regiment • Cow Neck Peninsula Historical Society

## Posters

War posters, concise in message and graphically different, had great impact. Famous artists ran war poster art classes and competitions. New York's Public Library was turned into a giant billboard for the Loan posters. In 1918, 19 million posters were distributed just for Liberty Loans.

**Above:** Howard Chandler Christy's 3rd Liberty Loan poster, 1918, depicting Columbia, female symbol of U.S.

**Above:** Joseph Pennell's 4th Liberty Loan poster, "That Liberty Shall Not Perish from the Earth", 1918, portraying the Statue of Liberty in ruins and the New York skyline in flames.

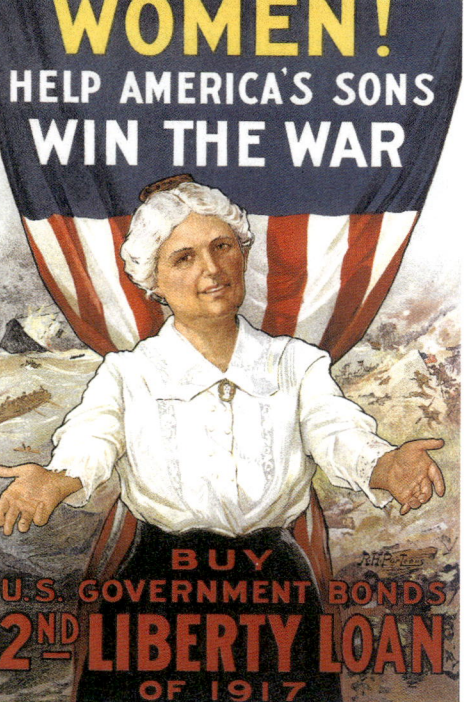

**Left:** R.H. Porteus' 2nd Liberty Loan poster, 1917, appealing to mothers.

## A Patriotic Duty

Liberty Loan Bonds and War Savings Stamps raised about $17 billion during 4 bond issues – needed, as WWI cost $30 billion. The stamps were sold in smaller amounts, some 25¢, yet made a billion dollars. Purchases yielded interest, a new concept to many. Elite Army pilots doing acrobatics and 4-Minute Men encouraged people. Bond rallies were held by movie stars, and in New York City, large structures, including a captured German submarine, were displayed.

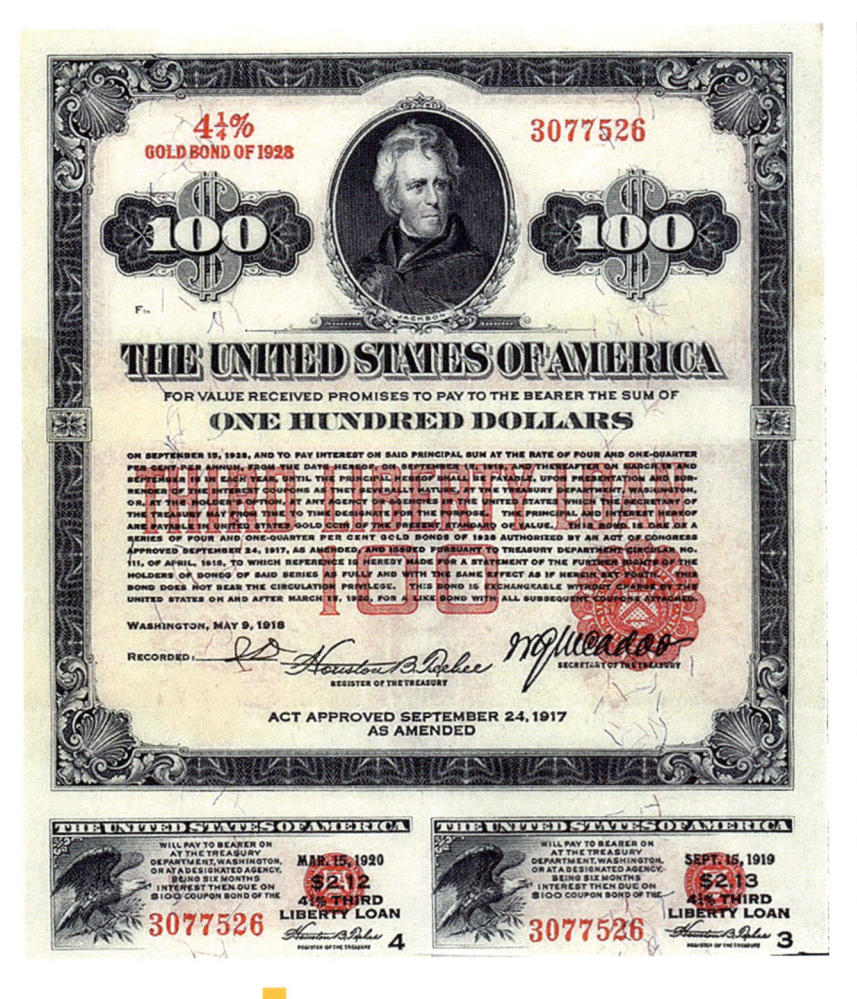

**Top:** Liberty Bond Certificate for $100 in 3rd Loan Campaign, with coupons for 6-month interest payments.

**Top:** New York Stock Exchange from steps of the Sub-Treasury during 4th Loan Campaign.

72  WWI: The Homefront • Regiment • Cow Neck Peninsula Historical Society

Above: Bond department at a leading bank during the rush to buy Liberty Loans.

Left: Post Office's postmark advertised loan; Red Cross added a rubber stamp.

Below: Poster depicting "financing democracy in its fight against despotism."

Left: Liberty Loan certificates were offered to immigrants of all nations in their own language.

## Our Community

- Mr. & Mrs. Daniel Guggenheim held a rally at their Hempstead House in Sands Point. They sold $500,000 in bonds, $100,000 to Mr. Guggenheim.
- Main Street's Bank of North Hempstead gave easy terms to buy a bond.
- A parade included Capt. Floherty's Company A, the Red Cross in uniform, Girl Pioneers with a flag as wide as the road, fire trucks, and Boy Scouts.
- Company A's loan drive put our town in 2nd place in Nassau County.

# Peach Pits and Gas Masks

The Girl Scouts collected pits of peaches, other fruits, and nutshells. The carbon in the pits was extracted to make charcoal filters for soldiers' gas masks. The Red Cross, Boy Scouts, schools, and movie theatres all participated. By the end of the war 4,000 tons of pits and shells had gone to the Long Island City Gas Mask Factory in Astoria.

## Peach Pit Project

The Girl Scouts, newly founded in 1912, stepped up their war efforts when we entered the war. They knitted, made jam, and sold Liberty Bonds. In fact, they sold over $3 million worth in the 3rd Liberty Loan Drive. They ran a successful campaign to collect peach pits.

### This Peach Pitter No Peach

Out in Port Washington, Long Island, the proprietor of the Nassau Theatre offered a weekly pass to any youngster who called at the box office with five pounds of peach-stones for the gas mask industry.

Two nights after this liberal offer had appeared upon the Nassau's screen Druggist Hunold of the same town missed the barrel which had been placed in front of his store for donated pits.

**Top:** The 3 D.C. preteen "Peach Pit Champions."
**Middle:** The Port News request yielded 700 lbs. of pits.
**Bottom:** Carbon from 200 peach pits made 1 filter.

WWI: The Homefront • Regiment • Cow Neck Peninsula Historical Society

## Gas Masks

In April 1915, the Germans fired 150 tons of poisonous green clouds of chlorine gas at the French in Ypres. It was the first time chemical weapons were used in conflict. Gas was heavy, ideally suited to gassing trenches and the wounded on the ground. Eyes were blinded, lungs swelled and burned, skin blistered inside and out. Terror and panic were rife. Chemical warfare caused over 1.3 million casualties and about 100,000 fatalities, mostly from phosgene, 6 times more deadly than chlorine gas.

> "…I was dazed, knocked down and my gas mask knocked off. I got several breaths of the strong solution right from the shell before it got diluted with much air…I gasped, choked and felt the extreme terror of the man who goes under in the water and will clutch at a straw."
>
> —W. Stull Holt, New York City-born driver with the American Ambulance Field Service, September 1, 1917, Verdun, France.

Weird-Looking Masks for Protection

**Above and right:** Gas spared no one. Soldiers, nurses, and support animals were all casualties. Masks and goggles had to be procured quickly. Oftentimes dogs and horses were not given goggles to protect their eyes and were blinded.

**Right:** World War I gas mask, top. World War II gas mask with chemical warfare cape, carrying pouch, and "anti-dimming" de-fogging cloth in tin.

WWI: The Homefront • Regiment • Cow Neck Peninsula Historical Society

# Save Your Coal!

We had a coal shortage even before we entered the war. Now, even more coal was needed. Fuel costs became regulated at all levels of processing: the mines, the docks and railways, the end users. Work weeks were shortened except for war-related factories. Heatless Mondays were instituted. Daylight Savings Time was put into effect on March 31, 1918, in an attempt to curtail fuel usage.

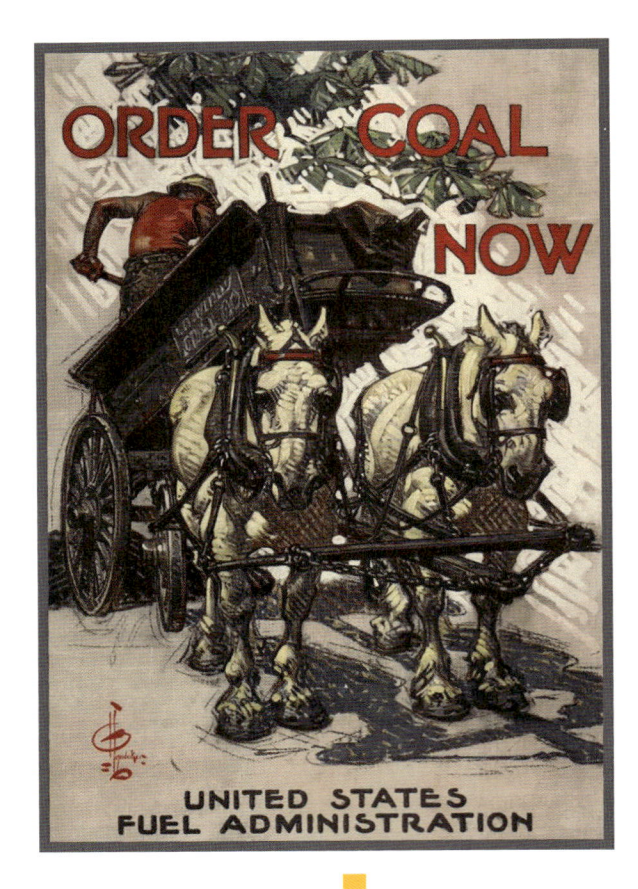

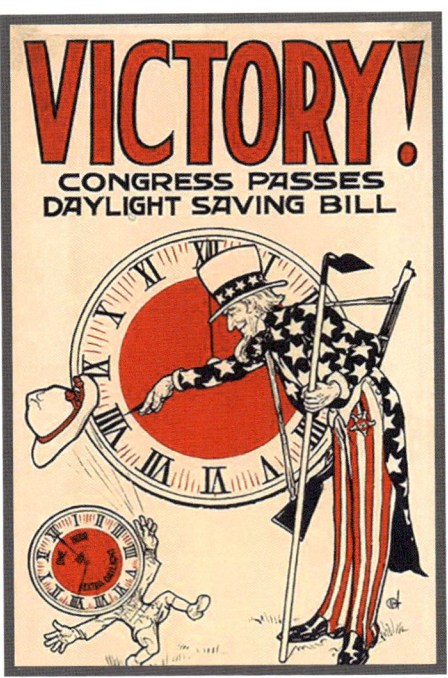

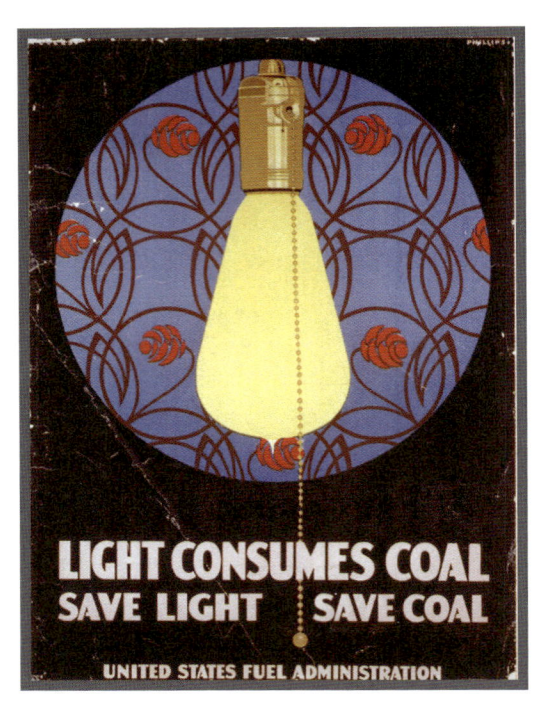

Three Fuel Savings Posters for Coal, Daylight Saving, and Lighting.

The Tagger Will Get You

**Left:** Reading Times, January 30, 1918
**Below:** Coal Shovel Tag, reverse side.

**HINTS ON SAVING COAL**
1. Cover furnace and pipes with asbestos, or other insulation; also weather strip your windows, or stuff cracks with cotton.
2. Keep your rooms at 68° (best heat for health).
3. Heat only the rooms you use all the time.
4. Test your ashes by sifting. If you find much good coal, there is something wrong with your heater. See a furnace expert.
5. Write to the maker of your furnace or stove for practical directions for running economically.
6. Save gas and electric light as much as possible—this will save coal for the nation.

U. S. FUEL ADMINISTRATION

## Shovel Tagging Campaign

Over 21 million school children and Boy Scouts participated in a national movement on January 30, 1918: "Tag Your Shovel Day!" Children were given a special national holiday. Two large printing plants produced tags that read, "Save that shovelful of coal a day for Uncle Sam." Coal-saving tips were on the reverse to encourage people to save a few pounds of coal. The children visited homes to tag shovels everywhere, including President Wilson's shovel at the White House.

Jan. 30th Tag your shovel DAY
has your Coal shovel been tagged yet?
UNITED STATES FUEL ADMINISTRATION

**Left:** Coal Shovel Poster.
**Below:** Tagged coal shovel and coal scuttle.

WWI: The Homefront • Regiment • Cow Neck Peninsula Historical Society

WWI: The Homefront • Regiment • Cow Neck Peninsula Historical Society

# In Our Spare Time . . .

**"The Wool Brigades of World War I, When Knitting Was a Patriotic Duty"**

"People knitted not just at home but at work, at church, on public transport, in the theatre, and while waiting for trains and sitting in restaurants…In 1915, the New York Philharmonic Society had to issue a plea for audience members to refrain from knitting, as it disrupted performances"

—Anika Burgess, Atlas Obscura

# Everyone Must Knit!— Knit Your Bit!

Knitting became a patriotic duty for everyone, young and old, male and female. Different organizations lured people with colorful tape measures and knitting bags, and water-repellant wool was promoted to better protect the soldiers.

In 1919, in Madison Square, hundreds of working women assembled at lunchtime to knit. 30 miles north of New York City, "prisoners knit in the yard at Sing Sing while listening to a concert by the mandolin club."

– Anika Burgess, Atlas Obscura

The American Red Cross estimated that 370 million knitted items were made between 1917 and 1919.

**Top, left:** Khaki Knitting Book, adorned with Allies' flags. The American Red Cross and Navy League provided knitting patterns for uniformity in soldier's items.

**Top, right:** Sock Rule. To prevent frostbite, trench-foot, and blisters when wool reserves got low, everyone was told to just knit socks using patterns printed in magazines.

**Above:** Central Park's 1918 3-Day Knitting Bee was very well-attended and featured contests of all types, yielding 224 pairs of socks, 50 sweaters, and 40 balaclavas.

**Bottom:** John Singer Sargent's oil painting, "Gassed," 1919, depicts soldiers blinded after a mustard gas attack. Eye bandages were knit to protect soldiers' eyes.

WWI: The Homefront • Regiment • Cow Neck Peninsula Historical Society

## WWI Quilt

Homemade textiles for both soldiers and civilians were created during WWI, from knitted items to apparel to "sweetheart" pillows to this quilt.

This image is of a WWI Quilt in the Collections of The Henry Ford Museum. It is a unique 72" square quilt of cotton, wool, and flannel, with appliqué and embroidering, in olive green, red, white, and blue, with wartime inscriptions. The National WWI Museum and Memorial adds that the quilt is made from mass-produced service banners, available at stores like Woolworth. There was no standard for service star banner production, so there were many variations in fabric.

The quilt was designed and made by Herbert James Smith, a lifelong tailor. He lived for a time in San Francisco, near the Presidio Army Base, where General Pershing made his home. Smith was reputed to have made uniforms for the General, and the 1920 U.S. Census listed his occupation as military tailor.

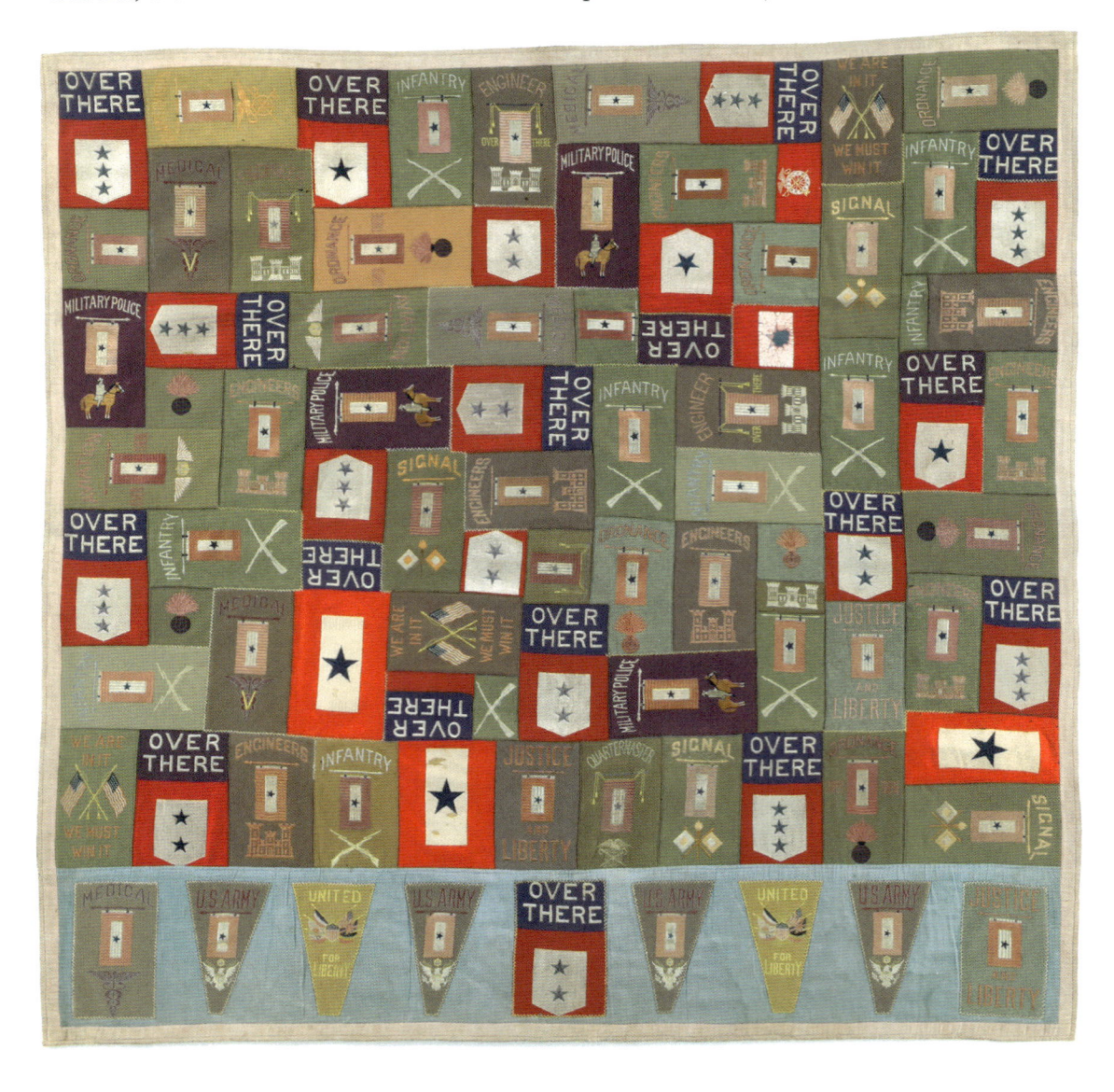

From the Collections of The Henry Ford Museum

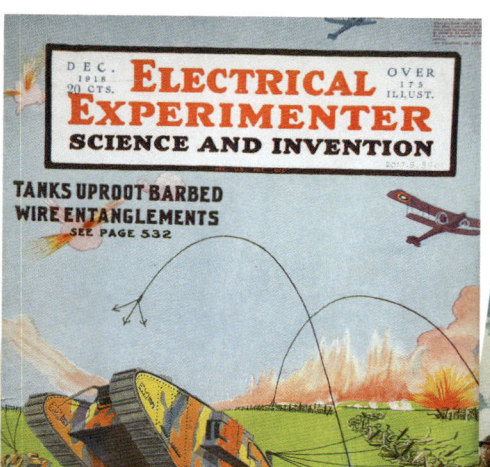

**Below:** "Ladies Home Journal" often featured war-related cover art like this photograph of soldiers and was filled to the brim with content on the war effort.

**Above, left:** A Red Cross war service dog decorated with the French Croix de Guerre, for services of valor and distinction, was on this cover of Ladies Home Journal.

**Above, center:** "Electrical Experimenter Science and Invention" had a trove of new warfare inventions for their articles and colorful covers.

**Right:** Harvard Lampoon editor Edward Streeter turned his comical "Dere Mable" letters from a successful column into a series of illustrated books.

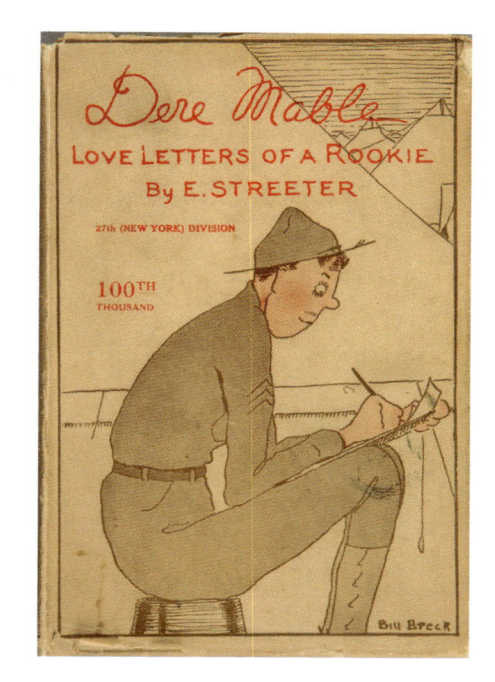

## Publications

The written word was the means of communication in WWI. Television had not been invented and all civilian radio activity, still in its early years, was shut down in 1917 for the duration of the war. It was illegal to own a radio transmitter or receiver; usage was treasonous.

Newspapers and magazines provided news of the war and information on joining the war effort. People read of the troops' progress, with photographs and maps. Reading frontline soldier's letters and war stories were popular. Opportunities to join home front organizations were published, as were patriotic advertisements. New ways to garden, cook, and sew were given.

WWI: The Homefront • Regiment • Cow Neck Peninsula Historical Society

# The Music of WWI

Three renditions of "Over There," written by George M. Cohan, made the top 12 song list of 1917, with one recording in first place. Popular war songs raised the morale of civilians and soldiers, as did patriotic songs. "The Star-Spangled Banner," not yet the National Anthem, and "The Battle Hymn of the Republic" made the top lists as well. Our country's changing viewpoints during the war years could be monitored by themes of songs:

- 1915: "I Didn't Raise My Boy to Be a Soldier"
- 1916: "America – My Country, 'Tis of Thee"
- 1917: "Pack Up Your Troubles in Your Old Kit Bag"
- 1918: "Hail, Hail, The Gang's All Here"
- 1919 - #1: "Till We Meet Again"

## John Philip Sousa

When WWI broke out, American composer-conductor John Philip Sousa was commissioned as Lieutenant of the Naval Reserve Band, despite being 62, the mandatory retirement age for officers. "The March King," who wrote 136 military marches, had been director of the U.S. Marine Band and his own band.

He now wrote marches supporting the war or honoring those who did. The many beneficiaries included the Army, shipbuilders, and the Liberty Loan. When the war ended, Sousa paid tribute to those who died, like Theodore Roosevelt's son Quentin, who was killed in aerial combat, and dedicated the moving march that included "Taps," to Theodore Roosevelt's wife Edith Roosevelt.

Sousa, promoted to lieutenant commander, received the WWI Victory Medal. He was very proud of his Navy service and wore his Navy uniform throughout his life.

Mr. Sousa lived in Sands Point, at *Wild Bank*, from 1912 until his death in 1932. Still a private residence, it is a National Historic Landmark. Our town remembers him at both the Memorial Bandshell and the elementary school that bear his name.

**Left:** "New Victor Records publication, March 1918.

## Irving Berlin

In 1917, songwriter Irving Berlin was drafted into the Army and stationed at Camp Upton. There he wrote, "Oh, How I Hate to Get Up in the Morning," a comic portrayal of military life.

Encouraged by the Army, he then composed an all-soldier musical, "Yip-Yip-Yaphank." The next year the show went to Broadway. During the finale, the main performers marched down the aisle and out of the theatre. In September 1918, Sgt. Irving Berlin and the entire 300-person crew marched out of the theatre for the last time. They were on their way to France.

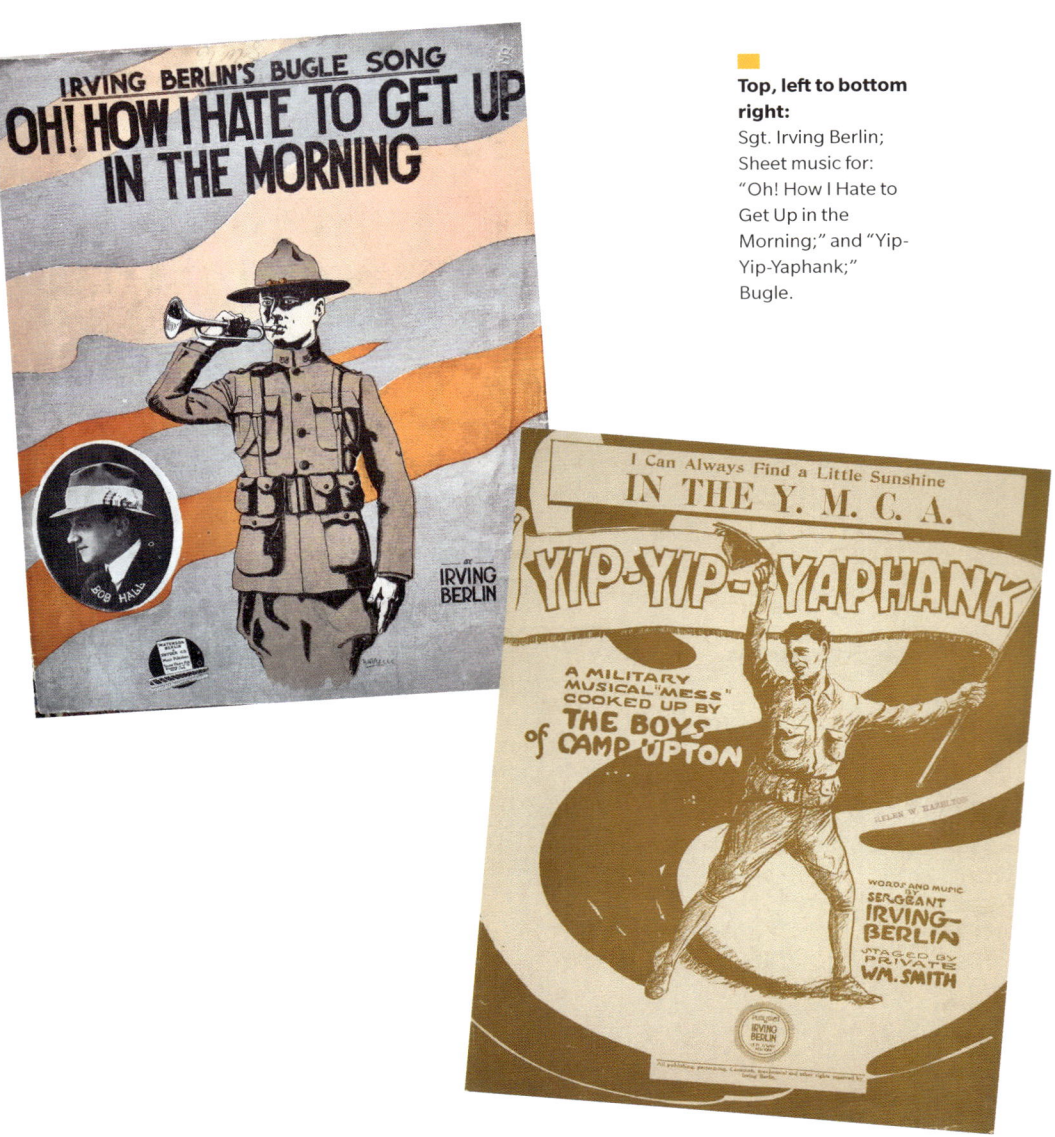

**Top, left to bottom right:**
Sgt. Irving Berlin; Sheet music for: "Oh! How I Hate to Get Up in the Morning;" and "Yip-Yip-Yaphank;" Bugle.

88 WWI: The Homefront • Regiment • Cow Neck Peninsula Historical Society

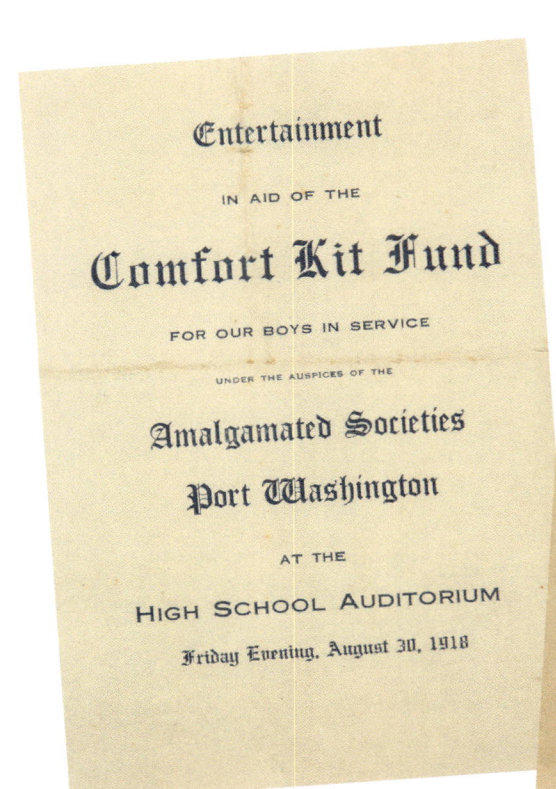

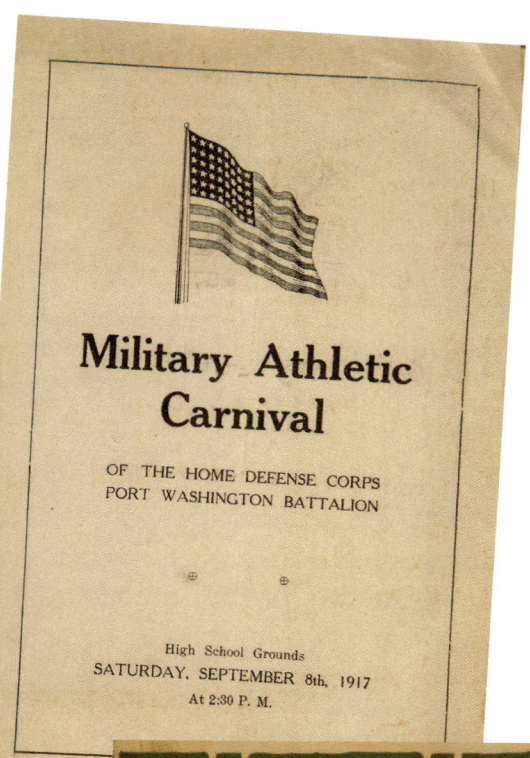

## Notable Port Washington WWI Events

*A Musical Evening:* Entertainment in aid of the Comfort Kit Fund for our boys in service under the auspices of the Amalgamated Societies, Port Washington at the High School Auditorium, Friday evening, August 30, 1918.

*Athletic Competitions:* Military Athletic Carnival of the Home Defense Corps, Port Washington Battalion, High School Grounds, Saturday, September 8th, 1917, at 2:30 P.M.

*Port Washington Home Guard Event:* "A" Company Minstrel Show, Nassau Theatre, December Fourteenth, 1917.

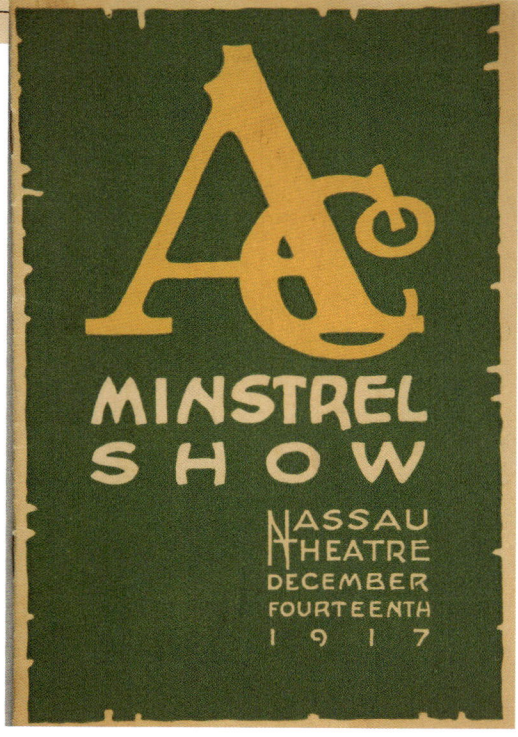

All of the above:
— From the CNPHS Collection

# Trench Art

Only the smallest pieces of trench art were likely made at the front line. Larger and more secure trenches had images and words sculpted into the walls, but most trenches were waterlogged and filled with mud, rats, louses, debris, and wounded and dying men. The war rained down on them and soldiers had little room to keep their possessions secure.

Decorated shell casings were the most common form of trench art. The metal was beaten or engraved with designs, and often the site and year was etched on.

It is probable that art made from shell casings and other war debris was done behind the line in workshops by soldiers, by civilians in their homes, by the convalescing, and by prisoners-of-war. The items were made or bought by soldiers as remembrances, souvenirs, or gifts.

Trench art WWI poppy vase.
—On loan from Susan Murphy

Trench art 3-footed vase, embossed with "Yser" (Belgium). On bottom, "Febr 1918 Magdeburg" (Germany).
—On loan from CNPHS Trustees Jennifer and Colin Wiggins

**Bottom, left:** Trench art lighter, engraved "Verdun 1918."
—From CNPHS Collection

**Middle:** Trench art WWI matchbox cover, owner Martin Cocks.
—Donated by Janet Cocks Chudd

**Far right:** Trench art ring, decorative inlaid flags and staffs, French flag to the left, Belgian to the right. The years 1914 to 1917 are commemorated.
—On loan from CNPHS Treasurer Kenneth J. Buettner

90  WWI: The Homefront • Regiment • Cow Neck Peninsula Historical Society

**Far left:** Photo of discarded shell casings that littered the landscape.

**Near left:** Undecorated piece of shell casing, 1917
—Donated by Susan Murphy

## Stereoscopes

Using a stereoscope, two photos from slightly different angles are seen by each eye separately, allowing the viewer to see a 3-D image. The curve of the cardboard with images aids in the effect. It allowed folks back home to see what was happening in the war.

**Top:** "General Pershing Decorating Officers of 89th Division, Treves."

**Bottom:** "Thousands Marching – Our National Army."

**Right:** "America's Unknown Soldier Comes Home to his Native Soil," loaded onto stereoscope.
—Stereoscope from CNPHS Collection; Stereoscopic cards on loan from Trustees Jennifer and Colin Wiggins

WWI: The Homefront • Regiment • Cow Neck Peninsula Historical Society

# Mail Call!

Army Post Offices (APOs) distributed all mail from America – 35 million letters were delivered overseas to soldiers in one year alone. APOs sent return mail home for free for military men, but initially not for military women. Sensitive material was to be avoided; censorship was in effect.

An assortment of patriotic postcards to mail overseas.

**Below, left:** Authorization for supplies for Daniel White from official welfare organization. Atop is his French Croix de Guerre medal.

**Below, right:** Letter to Singleton Mitchell of Plandome suggesting purchase of 3% U.S. Treasury Notes "at cost." U.S. Treasury Dept. envelope stamped, "Your Patriotic Duty – Buy a Liberty Loan Bond.

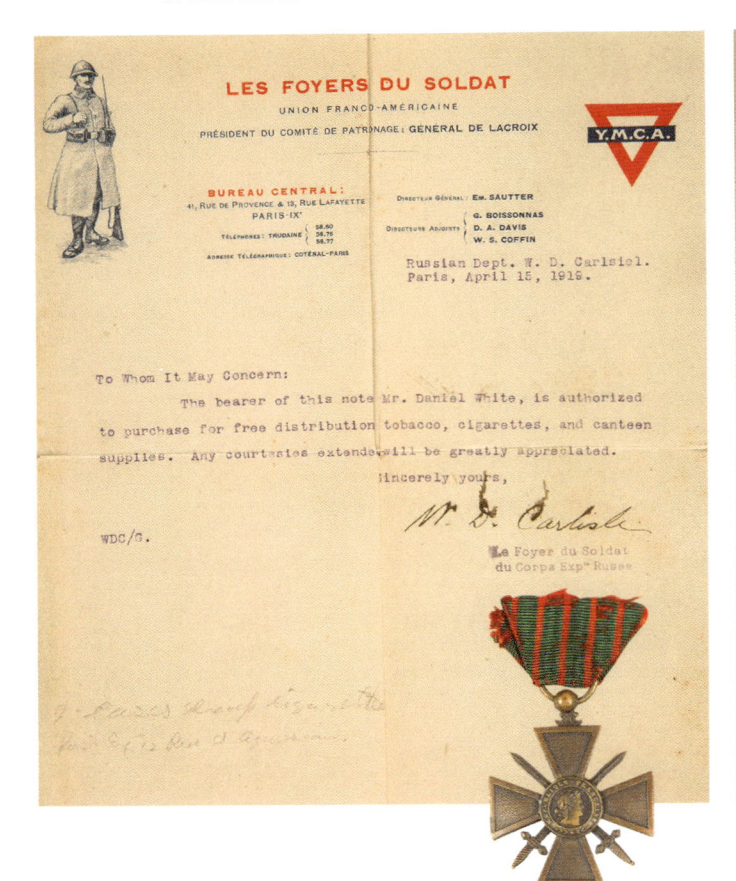

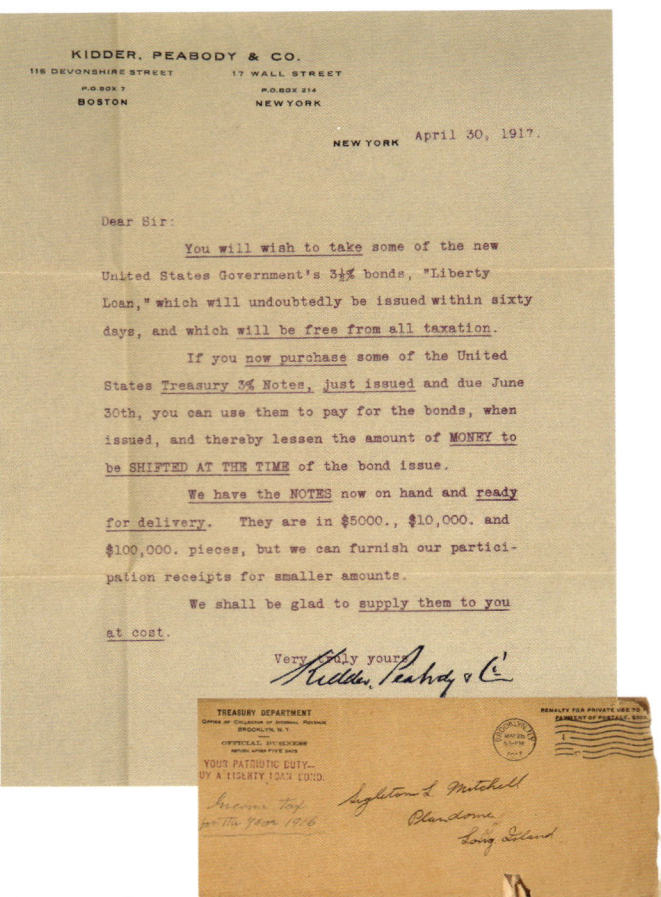

92  WWI: The Homefront • Regiment • Cow Neck Peninsula Historical Society

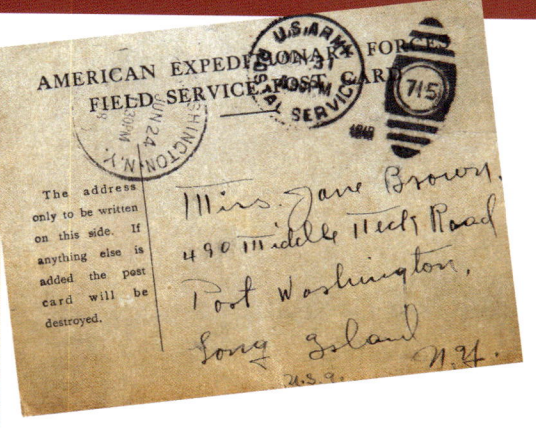

**Left, and above:**
2 A.E.F. Post Cards to Miss Jane Brown of Port Washington from Henry Bowyer. Optional sentences; one drew a line through sentences not pertinent. Only dates and a signature could be inserted or the post card would be destroyed.
—On Loan from Trustees Jennifer and Colin Wiggins

Jewish Welfare Board Post Card "Just Got Back." Men added in their Camp address, this one Camp Mills. Atop is Camp Mills token with double triangle on reverse.
—Post Card from CNPHS Collection; Token donated by Susan Murphy

Victory Medal and its mailing envelope. 14 Allied countries awarded such a medal to their nationals.

Censored postcards from France with locations scratched off and cut out.

Sweetheart card "from Harry," to his wife Julia.

Photographic post card of Sgt. Harry Wiggins performing foot inspections.
—All on Loan from Trustees Jennifer and Colin Wiggins; From Colin's grandfather's WWI collection.

WWI: The Homefront • Regiment • Cow Neck Peninsula Historical Society   93

Port Washington High School, Main Street, Port Washington, L. I.

# Education

## Wartime propaganda was prevalent in the schools.

In 1917 New York teachers had to sign loyalty oaths and teach citizenship courses that reflected the government's version of the war measures. Some lost their jobs for refusing to support slanted views, and many left their jobs before they were fired.

### In High Schools
The study plan for troops was taught: the virtues of the Americans and Allies vs. the dangers of Germans.

### In Universities
Male students were made uniformed army privates and had compulsory military education at some colleges and universities. A "War Issues Course" was offered, depicting Germany as the causal factor of all European problems historically.

# In Port Washington

Teachers and students alike seemingly supported the war effort with great loyalty and patriotism. Students were active in the Red Cross, learned business skills for civil service jobs, and raised money for soldiers' supplies, and the boys ramped up their physical training and military drill.

**Paul D. Schreiber**, principal of Port's High School on Main Street, was drafted in the spring of 1918. Students and teachers met him and his new wife at the railroad station to bid him farewell.

But a student waving a paper ran from the telegraph office. The students had secretly petitioned the draft board requesting a deferment for their principal until after commencement, and the approval just arrived. Principal Schreiber was hoisted atop the shoulders of his students, and the cheering crowd marched off.

Once in service, Private Schreiber suprised his students in November with a visit following a three-week school closure due to the influenza epidemic. He was reinstalled as principal once out of the service in early 1919.

**Top:** Paul D. Schreiber, Principal, Port Washington High School, 1917-1920, and Superintendent of Schools, 1921–1953.

**Right:** Paul D. Schreiber High School. (Photo: Wikimedia Creative Commons)

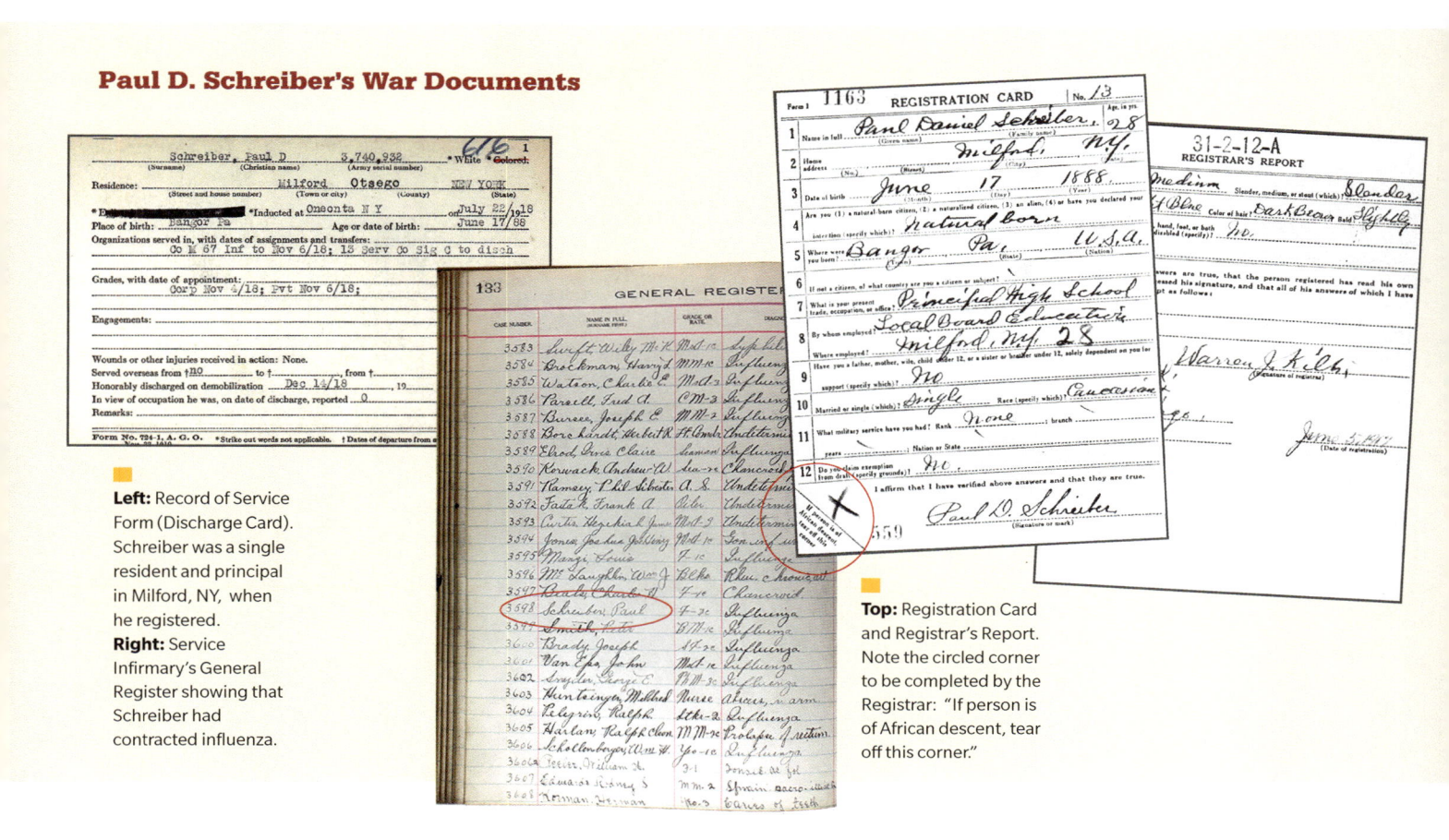

## Paul D. Schreiber's War Documents

**Left:** Record of Service Form (Discharge Card). Schreiber was a single resident and principal in Milford, NY, when he registered.

**Right:** Service Infirmary's General Register showing that Schreiber had contracted influenza.

**Top:** Registration Card and Registrar's Report. Note the circled corner to be completed by the Registrar: "If person is of African descent, tear off this corner."

WWI: The Homefront • Regiment • Cow Neck Peninsula Historical Society    **95**

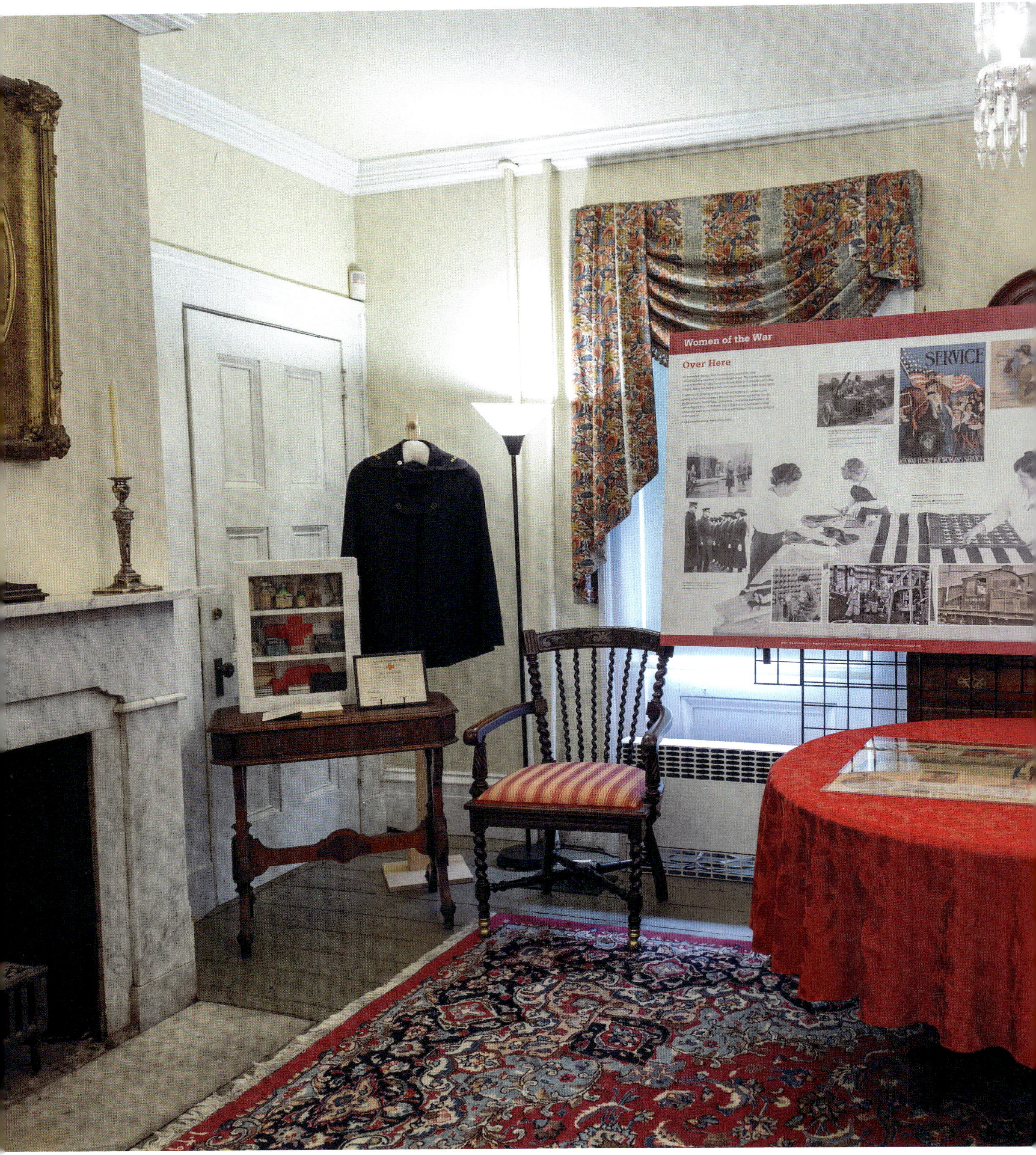
Women of the War
Over Here
SERVICE

# The Women Who Served

**"Hello Girls"**

"The work was fascinating; much of it was in codes changed frequently…'Toul' might be 'Podunk' one day and 'Wabash' the next…The girls had to speak both French and English and they also had to understand American Doughboy French."

—Grace D. Banker, Chief Operator of the U.S. Signal Corps' women telephone operators

# Women of the War: Over Here

Women of all classes, from housewives to socialites, were wholeheartedly involved in supporting the war. They performed jobs vacated by the men who had gone to war, both in civilian life and in the military. Many felt their patriotic service would secure them more rights.

In addition to growing and canning food, knitting for soldiers, and raising great sums of money, thousands of women worked as nurses, postal workers, firefighters, conductors, mechanics, bank tellers, camouflage artists, in factories, and in the military. Some performed dangerous work as munitions workers and Radium Girls, many dying of overexposure.

If a job needed doing, the women did it.

**Right, above:** Red Cross Motor Corps giving aid to Army, Navy, civilians, in influenza epidemic.

**Right, below:** Navy women's inspection, 1918.

**Below:** The New York Navy Yard's factory workers making flags, 1917.

**Above starting left:**
Woman factory welder.
Woman foundry workers.
Woman train engineer, Bush Terminal, Brooklyn, 1917.

Women's Machine Gun Squad, NYC, testing Lewis machine guns before sending to the front.

WWI: The Homefront • Regiment • Cow Neck Peninsula Historical Society

# Women of the War: Over There

Thousands of women volunteered for the Red Cross, Salvation Army, YWCA, and other organizations that could not have functioned without them. Women worked as shells flew and gas was unleashed.

They were ambulance drivers and provided food near the front lines. They operated canteens, and recreation and religious huts, and served as telephone operators, translators, and war correspondents.

Army, Navy, and Red Cross nurses treated deadly infections and wounds, burns from gas, and dying influenza patients. Many of these brave women perished.

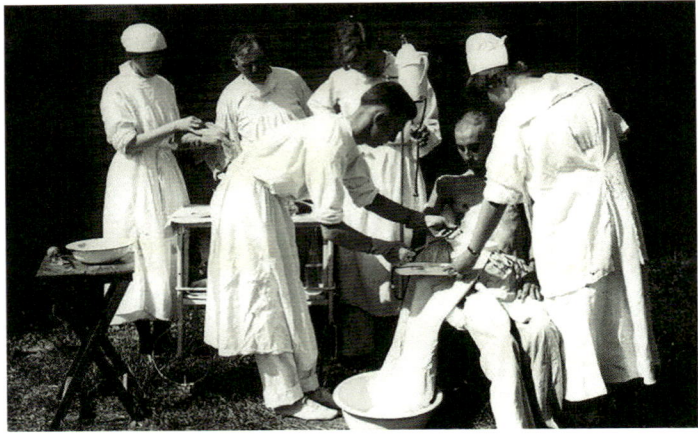

**Clockwise starting at top row, right:** YWCA's Frances Gulick, cited for valor and courage during aerial bombardment.

Nurses and doctors working in poor conditions.

Signal Corps "Hello Girls" transformed military communications that weren't working.

YWCA "Help Our Women War Workers" poster.

YWCA "Donut Lassies" treating injured soldiers in the trenches to a taste of home.

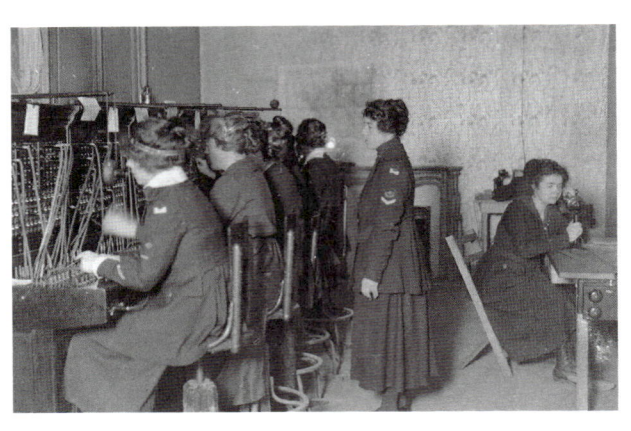

100 WWI: The Homefront • Regiment • Cow Neck Peninsula Historical Society

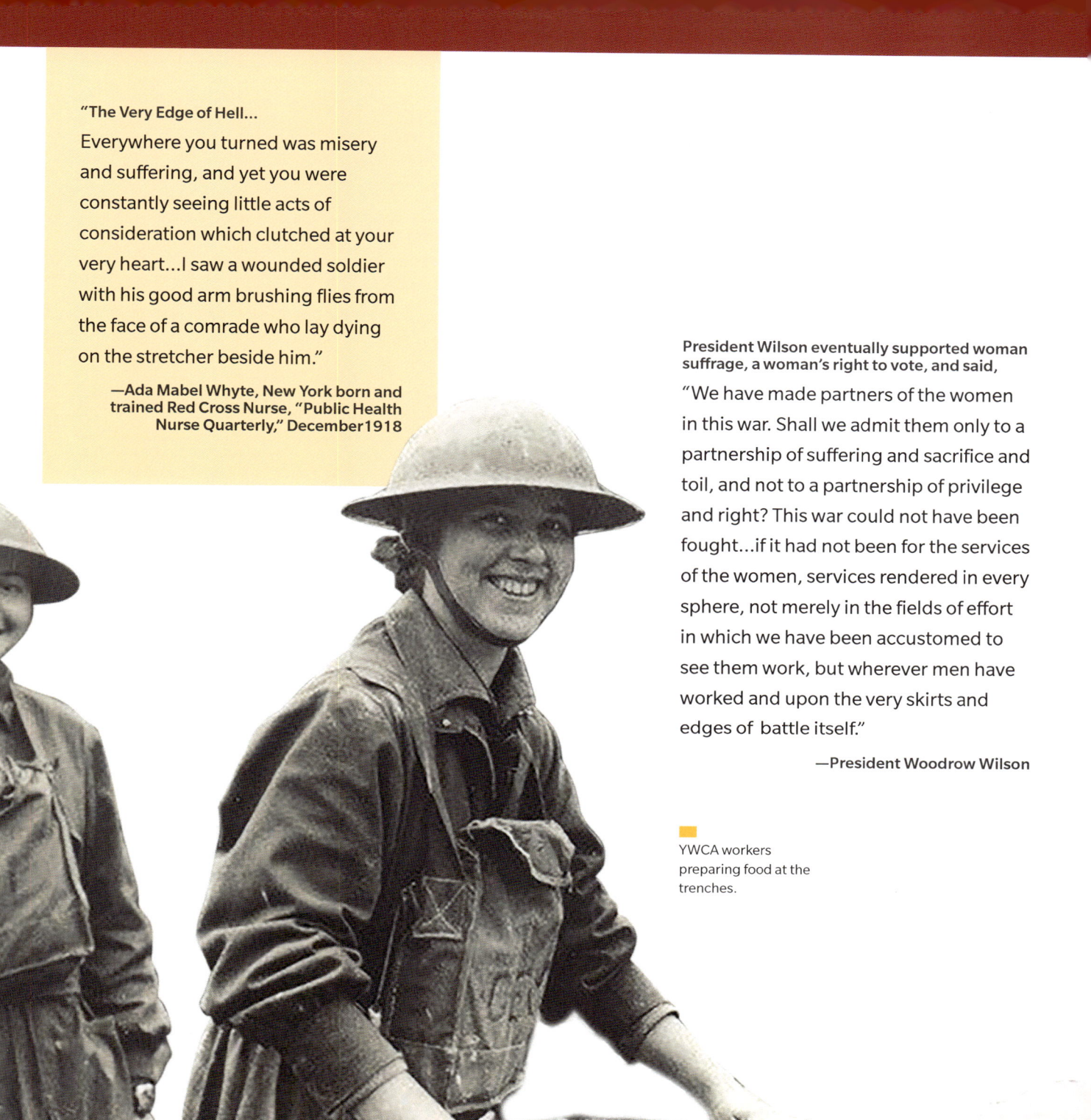

"**The Very Edge of Hell...**
Everywhere you turned was misery and suffering, and yet you were constantly seeing little acts of consideration which clutched at your very heart...I saw a wounded soldier with his good arm brushing flies from the face of a comrade who lay dying on the stretcher beside him."

—Ada Mabel Whyte, New York born and trained Red Cross Nurse, "Public Health Nurse Quarterly," December 1918

**President Wilson eventually supported woman suffrage, a woman's right to vote, and said,**

"We have made partners of the women in this war. Shall we admit them only to a partnership of suffering and sacrifice and toil, and not to a partnership of privilege and right? This war could not have been fought...if it had not been for the services of the women, services rendered in every sphere, not merely in the fields of effort in which we have been accustomed to see them work, but wherever men have worked and upon the very skirts and edges of battle itself."

—President Woodrow Wilson

YWCA workers preparing food at the trenches.

WWI: The Homefront • Regiment • Cow Neck Peninsula Historical Society   **101**

# Women's Organizations

Women volunteered for nursing, food, clerical, and communications work in military and civilian groups, but there were also more unusual opportunities.

The Camouflage Corps was a group of 40 female artists in New York City that painted ambulances, tanks, and ships with confusing 'dazzle' camouflage.

Munitions factory workers, known as 'canaries' due to their yellow skin from handling TNT, had no safety measures. 400 women died from overexposure.

Women war correspondents worked as journalists and photographers on the front line telling stories from a different perspective than readers were used to.

**Below:** National League assisted Red Cross, set up dining halls, telegraphed, all 24/7.

**Above:** Navy League recruited 11,000+ women for clerical and communications positions.

**"Radium Girls"**

Women were employed to paint military watches with radium to glow green in the dark.

The girls were instructed to make a fine point on their paint brushes using their lips or tongues and asked, "Does this stuff hurt you?" Mr. Savoy [the manager] said that it wasn't dangerous, that we didn't need to be afraid.

Yet the men in the radium factory wore lead aprons and masks and used tongs to handle it.

The women lost their teeth and jaws, and the radiation poisoning ate holes into their disintegrating bones. The doctors said they had syphilis.

—Mae Cubberley, an instructor of the "Radium Girls"

# The American Red Cross

Over 8 million volunteers were in WWI Red Cross chapters. Those at home made medical supplies, organized knitting for the soldiers, and nursed the wounded. Overseas, they also nursed, did air raid duty, cared for orphans, translated, and transported wounded, in 25 countries. Female doctors, rejected by the Army, joined the Red Cross. Some in the field and war hospitals were bombarded, hundreds losing their lives.

**Above:** Red Cross cabinet containing a variety of early 20th century medical supplies; Post-WWI nursing cape. Cabinet donated by Chris Bain; supplies donated by Doris Markham and William Evans; nurse's cape donated by Gilda Tesoriero.

**pan·dem·ic /pan'demik/**
a disease prevalent over the world; a global epidemic.

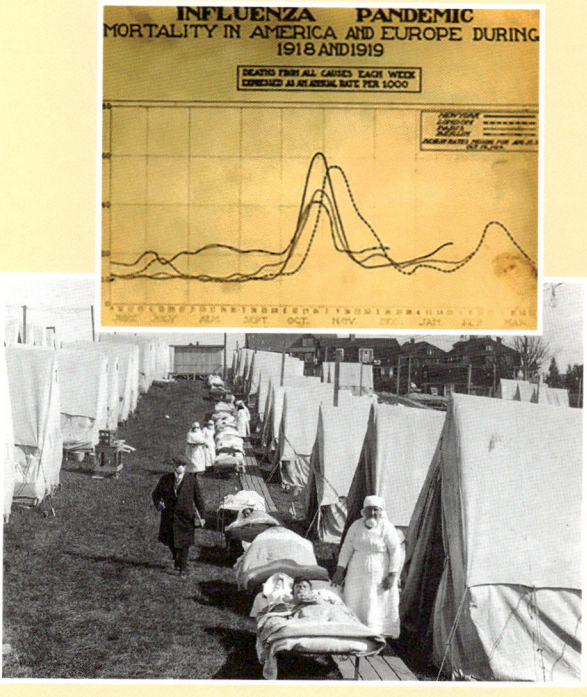

**Top to bottom:** New York City deaths surpassed European cities, 1918-1919. U.S. emergency tent hospitals were set up. Red Cross motor corps: 40 nurses made house calls to about 3,000. Quarantine notice to milkman.

WWI: The Homefront • Regiment • Cow Neck Peninsula Historical Society

# Influenza Pandemic

Reports of an influenza outbreak first came from neutral Spain in 1918, causing the virus to be dubbed, "The Spanish Flu," despite the fact that this epidemic may have originated in the United States. America was more concerned with the morale of the troops and the citizens on the home front. Prioritizing propaganda over public health hindered our ability to respond effectively to the deadly threat.

- 500 million people were infected - 1/3 of the world's population.
- 50,000,000 + deaths globally.
- 675,000 + deaths in the United States.
- In 1918, more died from the flu than as a result of the war.

**Spring 1918:**
# The First Wave

100 soldiers at Fort Riley, Kansas contracted the flu in March, and the number of cases quintupled in a week. There were no vaccines or antibiotics to help combat the flu. Overcrowding at camps and global troop travel greatly contributed to the spread of the disease.

**Fall 1918:**
# The Second Wave

Military sites near Boston were hit hard by this highly fatal second wave. 195,000 Americans died from the flu in October alone. Nursing shortages grew, worsened by a refusal to use African American nurses.

In New York City, the Board of Health required all flu cases to be isolated at home or in city hospitals. Street sweepers were engaged as grave diggers.

The average life expectancy in the United States fell by 12 years.

**Winter 1918—Spring 1919:**
# The Third Wave

A resurgence of influenza occurred as soldiers demobilized and Armistice Day was celebrated. Stores and factories staggered their working hours, and employees were encouraged to walk instead of using public transportation.

In the first 5 days of January, 1,800 flu cases and 101 deaths were reported in San Francisco, where judges held court outdoors. NYC reported 706 cases of flu and 67 deaths in January. New cases started to diminish in February through the summer.

**Winter 1919—Spring 1920:**
# The Fourth Wave

While not often reported, a Fourth Wave struck, but Americans were tired of taking precautions with masks, social distancing, and public closures. The Fourth Wave proved to be very lethal.

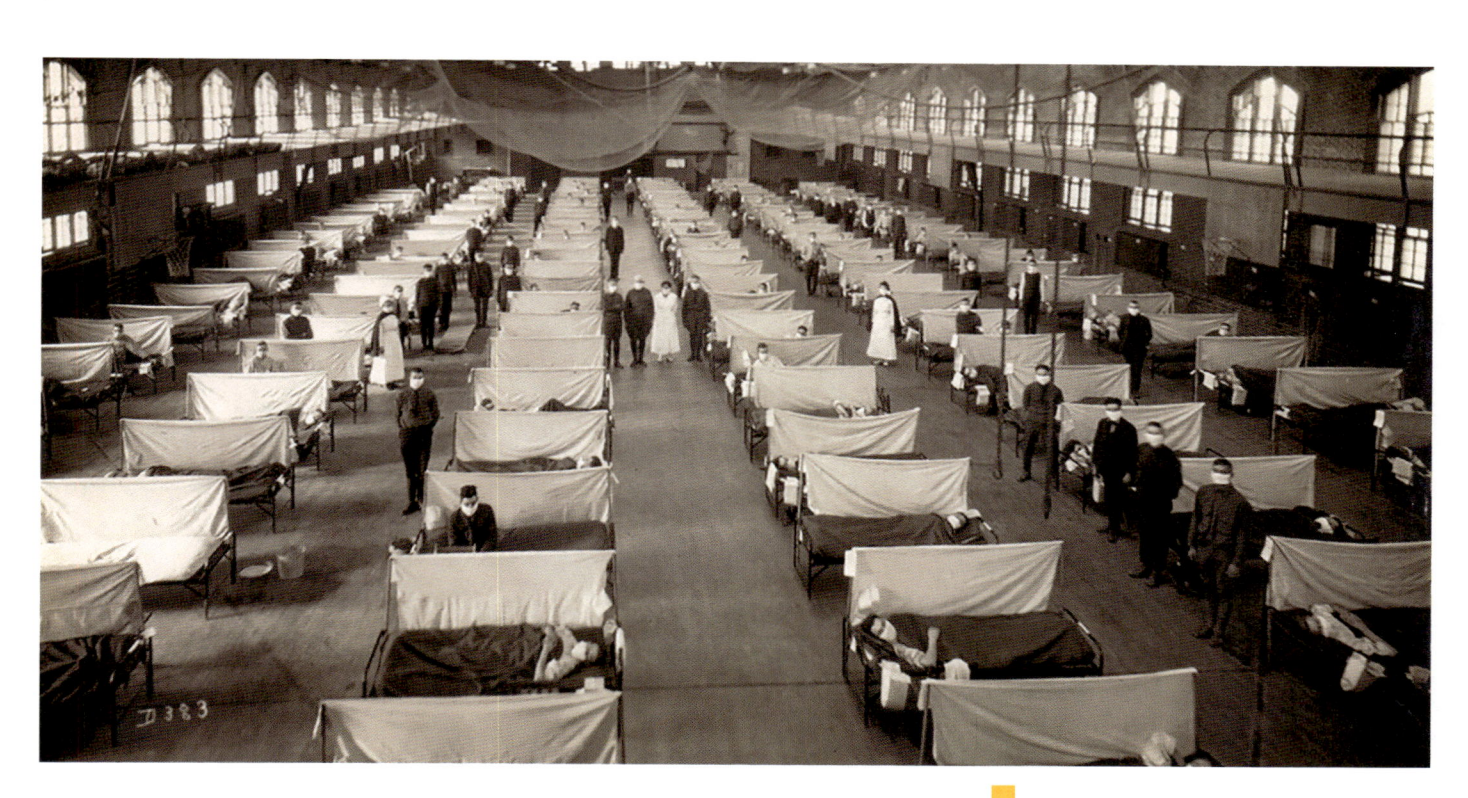

American makeshift emergency hospital for military influenza pandemic patients.

## Port Washington's Emergency Hospital

Prior to the influenza pandemic, Port Washington built an isolation hospital on Barkers Point on Goodwin-Gallagher Sand Mining land to combat the contagious outbreak of infantile paralysis (polio). When the U.S. entered WWI in 1917, a Red Cross storage facility was established there.

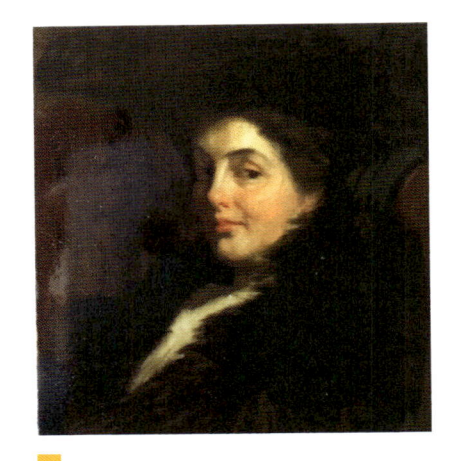

When the influenza epidemic struck in 1918, Port Washington turned to Mrs. Lillian Walker to set up a temporary emergency hospital on the site. She was chairwoman of the Military Relief Committee. Townspeople volunteered; in fact, in this Sands-Willets House, Mrs. Anna Willets Lapham cared for an 11-month old whose mother was in the hospital. The hospital was open for 6 weeks until the crisis subsided in late November.

Mabel Guest, born to a military family, was a registered nurse who enlisted in the Red Cross on September 6, 1918, and became head nurse. Feeling ill one day, she asked Mrs. Walker to leave work early, and she never returned. She had contracted influenza and died within a week on October 30, 1918.

Long Island did not escape the pandemic of 1918. In Port Washington, 59 people succumbed that year with 6 people dying in one week alone. The Town of North Hempstead recorded the deaths of 1,000 people from this highly contagious disease.

Mrs. Lillian Walker

Miss Mabel Guest

Port Washington Red Cross Unit marching in 1917 parade on Fifth Avenue and 42nd Street. Jane Brown Willkie at far right.

106 WWI: The Homefront • Regiment • Cow Neck Peninsula Historical Society

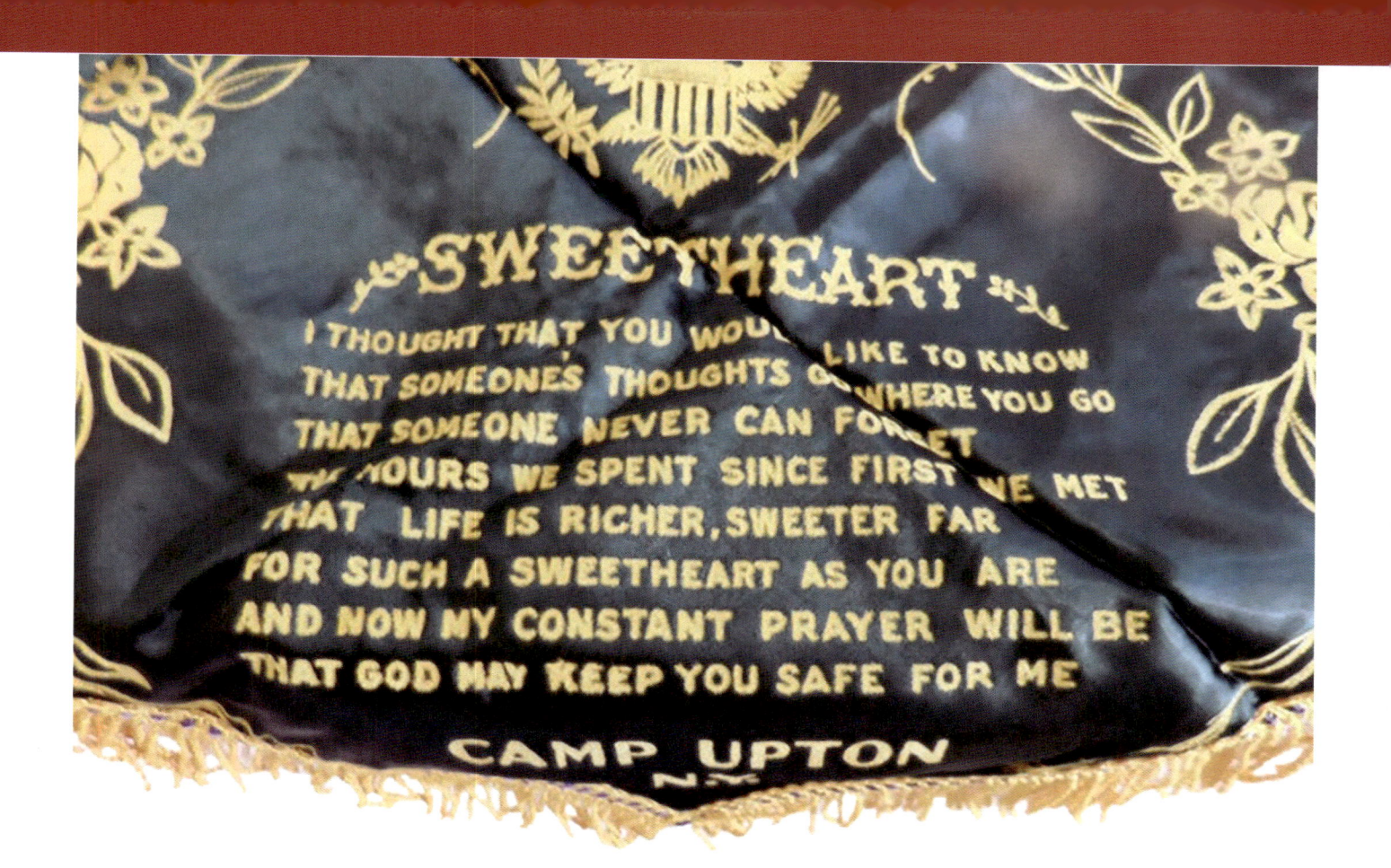

# Sweetheart Silks

Sweetheart pillows, silken pillows for letters, and embroidered hankies were made as keepsakes during WWI. Service men could purchase these lightweight remembrance gifts at military bases, both here and overseas, to send home to their sweethearts, wives, and mothers. These sweetheart silks became a cottage industry, often made by French and Belgian women to provide an income during the war.

# Silkens

Patriotic images and flowers were the most popular motifs for the silken remembrances, with the addition of poetry to a mother or sweetheart. Silken pincushions, often in the shape of a heart, and silk postcards were also available to the soldiers to send home to their loved ones.

**Top:** An assortment of silken handkerchiefs and a doily embroidered with poppies.
—From the CNPHS Collection

**Bottom:** A collection of silken sweetheart pillow shams, often patriotically embroidered.
—From the CNPHS Collection

108  WWI: The Homefront • Regiment • Cow Neck Peninsula Historical Society

Silken pillowed letter holders for holding special mail from one's sweetheart, closed and opened views.
 —From the CNPHS Collection

WWI: The Homefront • Regiment • Cow Neck Peninsula Historical Society    **109**

WWI: The Homefront • Regiment • Cow Neck Peninsula Historical Society

# The Men Who Served

**"Remember the Fourth"**

"In the midst of our welcome home ceremonies we must not forget those who gave their lives for the great cause. Their names will go down in history, and some day, we hope, Port Washington will honor the memory of these men as they should be honored."

—The Port Washington News, June 27, 1919

# The War is Finally Over

The guns fell silent on the 11th hour of the 11th day of the 11th month, ending the Great War, the war to end all wars.

It was only called **World War I** once there was a World War II.

**Premature armistice**
## November 7, 1918

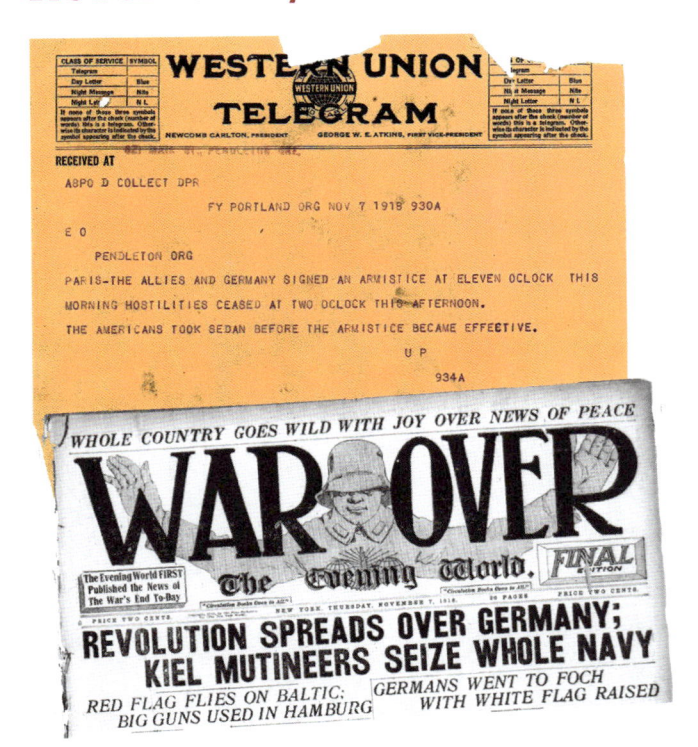

**Above, top:** A misinterpreted order had officers sending out misinformation via telegram.

**Above, bottom:** The Dow Jones ticker and telegraph and telephone lines spread the erroneous news in minutes. Newspapers put out extra editions.

**The Next Day**
## November 8, 1918

U.S. Army Intelligence later explained that a ceasefire order was issued to the front line to allow German Armistice Delegates to cross. The order, given days early, was to insure that all would receive the message. The order did not state its purpose, however, and intercepting officers assumed it was a general ceasefire.

**Above:** Premature Armistice, November 7, 1918.

### "Country Goes Wild on 'Fake' Report of End of War"

*"Port Washington Falls in Line with Big City in Celebrating Event Which is Yet to Take Place"*

—*The Port Washington News* Headline, November 8, 1918

112    WWI: The Homefront • Regiment • Cow Neck Peninsula Historical Society

**Real armistice**
# November 11, 1918

Our soldiers fought valiantly and much of our country supported them tirelessly.

- 4.7+ million Americans served.
- 116,516 military personnel died, over half from influenza.
- 500,000 New Yorkers served.
- 330+ from Port Washington served

**The New York Times**

**ARMISTICE SIGNED, END OF THE WAR! BERLIN SEIZED BY REVOLUTIONISTS; NEW CHANCELLOR BEGS FOR ORDER; OUSTED KAISER FLEES TO HOLLAND**

"How Port Washington Celebrated Victory"

"Apparently deciding that the premature celebration of last week was 'merely a dress rehearsal,' men, women and children of Port Washington went through a new delirium of joy at the news that the war is actually over. 'We had practice and we know how to do it now,' they cried. 'Let 'er go!'"

—The Port Washington News, November 15, 1918

**Top, right:** Ten days after Armistice, celebratory paper still covered the streets near City Hall Park, New York City, looking like snow.

**Left:** In cities and towns all across our nation thousands, like these Philadelphians on Broad Street, gathered to cheer on November 11th.

WWI: The Homefront • Regiment • Cow Neck Peninsula Historical Society   **113**

# Welcome Home!

**"Welcome Home to Our Boys"**

"…We parted from you with cheers; we greet you upon your return with cheers – and tears; cheers for those who survived and tears for those who sleep the immortal sleep of heroes in the lands they helped to save…"

—Richard Linthicum, The Port Washington News, July 4, 1919

New York City spared no expense in their expression of gratitude to those who served. The many tributes included:

**Left:** The Victory Arch, at Broadway and Fifth Avenue, completed the night before the 1st Welcome Home Parade on March 25, 1918. It was built as a temporary structure to commemorate deceased New Yorkers.

**Far left:** The Arch of Jewels, at Fifth Avenue and 60th Street, built of two 80' temporary shafts covered with thousands of prisms that sparkled with color when lit at night.

**Left:** One of two pyramids built outside of Grand Central Station of 85,000 German helmets sent home by General Pershing. The helmets were later sold for $1,000 each to raise funds for the Victory Loan; gun in foreground.

WWI: The Homefront • Regiment • Cow Neck Peninsula Historical Society

# Local Homecoming Parades

**Top, left:** Port Washington Fire Department marching on Main Street, Welcome Home Parade, July 4, 1919.
**Left:** Armistice Parade, photo by William H. Pickering in front of his store, 199 East Broadway, Roslyn.

**Top, right:** Port Washington Welcome Home Parade's band playing, traversing side streets throughout town.
**Below:** Joint welcome home celebration by Manhasset, Plandome, and Lakeville.

Towns across our nation celebrated the homecoming of their townspeople who served with parades and celebrations. Port Washington's activities included a parade, exercises at the high school grounds, a banquet for returning men, a baseball game at the high school diamond, and a block dance on South Washington Street, followed by fireworks.

MANHASSET — PLANDOME — LAKEVILLE
Homecoming and Memorial Celebration

SATURDAY, JUNE 21st, 1919

116   WWI: The Homefront • Regiment • Cow Neck Peninsula Historical Society

**Left:** "Our Heroes – Welcome Home" banner.
—From the CNPHS Collection

**Below:** "Our Heroes – Welcome Home" banner.
—On Loan from Margot Gramer

**Left:** "Welcome Veterans – World War Disabled American Veterans" banner.
—Donated by Susan Murphy

WWI: The Homefront • Regiment • Cow Neck Peninsula Historical Society

## Souvenir Program

**Souvenir Program**

The 'Welcome Home Day to the Men of Port Washington who served in the World War' was celebrated on July 4, 1919. The schedule of events for the day was noted and included the parade route through a dozen streets of town and the order of the groups marching. A Roll of Honor listed those who served, and an in memoriam page listed the deceased. Those organizing the event were mentioned, as were the Chairmen of the sponsoring Amalgamated Societies.

---

*Souvenir Program*

**Welcome Home Day**
To the Men of Port Washington who served in the WORLD WAR
JULY 4th, 1919

---

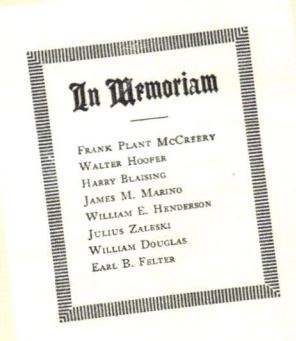

### PROGRAM

**Committee of Arrangements**
William C. Leiber, *Chairman*
Albert E. Gunn, *Secretary*
J. Henry Decker, *Treasurer*

9.30 A. M. Parade Forms At South Washington St.

11.00 A. M. Exercises At High School Grounds
- Singing of "Star Spangled Banner"
- Opening Address by Hon. Chas. R. Weeks
- Prayer by Rev. J. A. Carroll
- Address by Rev. Hubert A. Jones
- Address by Rev. Wm. J. Rutherford
- Address by Rev. George C. Groves
- Address by Hon. W. Bourke Cochran
- Presentation of Medals by Capt. Frederick S. Greene
- Singing "My Country 'Tis of Thee"
- Benediction by Rev. F. J. Muhlhauser

1.00 P. M. Banquet and Entertainment For Returning Men.
(At Strand Theatre)

3.00 P. M. Baseball Game—High School Diamond.
(Ushers Association vs. Philo Club of B'klyn)

8.30 P. M. Block Dance—South Washington Street.

10.00 P. M. Fireworks.

---

### In Memoriam

Frank Plant McCreery
Walter Hooper
Harry Blaising
James M. Marino
William E. Henderson
Julius Zaleski
William Douglas
Earl B. Felter

---

### ROLL OF HONOR

ALLEN, WESLEY
ALLEN, GEORGE
ALLEN, JOSEPH
ACCAHL, HAROLD S.
ALLEN, BERTRAM
ALSTON, THOMAS D.
BLAKE, MARTIN
BLUMBERG, JOHN J.
BIELER, CHARLES
BLAISING, HARRY G.
BROWER, LEONARD F.
BROWN, WALTER E.
BIATRYBRUSKI, KARMEN
BERKEL, WESLEY
BAKER, A. LEROY
BROWN, JOHN
BIDEON, WILLIAM
BENET, WILLIAM R.
BORER, ARTHUR
BROWNING, JOHN SCOTT
BOHAN, MATHEW
BROWN, WALTER E.
BIRKEL, EDWARD E.
BRYANT, CHARLES L.
BRAZIER, CHARLES A.
BIERMAN, ALBERT
BRENNEN, PATRICK
BINGEL, VICTOR
BLAKE, MICHAEL
BLAKE, PATRICK
BRADY, E. CLARK
BOLLERMAN, CHARLES M.
BUSWEILER, WILLIAM
BALDWIN, RICHARD
BORER, WILLIAM
BULLARD, J. E.
BALDWIN, WILLIAM, Jr.
BROWN, PHILIP
BIELER, CHARLES
CRAMPTON, JOSEPH
CROSS, LEONARD
CORRY, DOUGLAS
CHRISTENSEN, EDWARD
CHRISTENSEN, THOMAS
CIVEL, MICHAEL
CAMPAGNE, FRANK
CALIMORE, PHILIP
CHIPP, WILLIAM D.
CAPROCTA, PATRICK
CORRIGAN, JOHN
CALLAHAN, GEORGE
CARPENTER, CLARENCE

COCKS, HOWARD L.
CRAMPTON, EDWARD
CONKLIN, CHESTER
CONRAD, REGINALD
CONRAD, CLARENCE
COCKS, MARTIN J.
CORNWELL, DANIEL S.
CONRAD, WILFRED L.
CARPENTER, HARRY E.
CAREY, WILLIAM P.
DUNCAN, DAVID
DICKINSON, HARVEY J.
DICKINSON, ALFRED
DUSINBERRE, RALPH E.
DeMAR, SULLIVAN
DeMARTIN, HARRY
DUMPSON, HOWARD
DOUGLAS, WINFIELD
D'AGOSTINO, ANGELO D.
DOOLEY, WILLIAM .
DUNCAN, WM. BUTLER
DAY, WILLIAM S.
DeVOY, CLARENCE
DEVOE, ALBERT
DAVIS, ASHLEY
DiMEO, ROBERT
DARGAN, CHARLES A.
DEL SOLE, AUGIELLO
DiMEO, ALBERT
DiMEO, CHARLES
DURYEN, THOMAS J.
DALY, THOMAS
ERICKSON, JOHN
EVANS, W. H. Jr.
FRASER, THOMAS MOTT
FARNSWORTH, WILLIAM
FAVALE, RAFFAELI
FAY, JOSEPH
FRANCIS, JOSEPH
FATICONI, AMATO
FAY, ARTHUR
FORGONIE, LOUIS
FEARON, WILLIAM B. Jr.
GOULD, MAURICE
GRISCOM, WALTER
GRANT, GORDON
GREEN, FREDERICK S.
GALLAGHER, JOSEPH V.
GRAVEN, JOSEPH V.
GRIFFIN, EDWARD
GOODWIN, FRED

---

118    WWI: The Homefront • Regiment • Cow Neck Peninsula Historical Society

## ORDER OF PARADE

**LINE OF MARCH**

South Washington Street north to Main Street, east to Middle Neck Road, south to Bernard Street, west to Maryland Avenue, north to Main Street, west to Railroad Avenue, south to Franklin Avenue, west to Mackey Avenue, south to Murray Avenue, west to Main Street, north and east to High School Grounds.

SHERIFF'S RESERVES
SERVICE FLAG—CARRIED BY BOY SCOUTS AND PIONEER GIRLS
COLORS
BAND
CIVIL WAR VETERANS
SPANISH WAR VETERANS
WOUNDED BOYS IN CARS
CAPT. F. S. GREENE—MAJOR F. S. LAWRENCE
BOYS IN SERVICE
COLUMBIA COUNCIL NO. 51, JR. O. U. A. M.
PORT WASHINGTON COUNCIL, K. OF C.
AMERICA COUNCIL, D. OF L.
MARGUERITE REBEKAH LODGE, I. O. O. F.
YOUNG WOMAN'S RECREATION LEAGUE
VILLAGE WELFARE SOCIETY
ST. PETERS FIFE AND DRUM CORPS
ST. PETERS HOLY NAME SOCIETY
SEAWANHAKA LODGE NO. 670, I. O. O. F.
PORT WASHINGTON BRANCH NO. 1152—U. B. OF C. AND J.
DEMOCRATIC SOCIAL CLUB
BUSINESS MEN'S ASSOCIATION
ITALIAN BAND
ITALIAN AMERICAN POLITICAL SOCIETY
PORT WASHINGTON ITALIAN MUTUAL SOCIETY
POLISH SOCIETY
CHIEF MONTROVILLE SMITH AND BOARD OF FIRE DEPT.
ATLANTIC HOOK AND LADDER COMPANY
PROTECTION ENGINE COMPANY
FLOWER HILL HOSE COMPANY
NASSAU HOSE COMPANY
CITIZENS

## AMALGAMATED SOCIETIES
### OF PORT WASHINGTON

Thos. E. Roeber, *Chairman*   Albert E. Gunn, *Secretary*
J. Henry Decker, *Treasurer*

**INDEPENDENT ORDER ODD FELLOWS**
Chas. F. Lawrence, Chairman   B. J. Thompson

**JUNIOR ORDER UNITED AMERICAN MECHANICS**
John E. Hedges   William B. Fearon   Fred. W. Hamon

**PORT WASHINGTON REPUBLICAN CLUB**
J. H. Decker   Arthur W. Jones

**DEMOCRATIC SOCIAL CLUB**
Edward Dalton   Judge Roeber   Clarence E. Devoy

**ATLANTIC HOOK LADDER HOSE COMPANY**
William E. Lieber   T. O. Broadrick   W. V. Pearsall

**FLOWER HILL HOSE COMPANY**
John Finn   Fred Schlothauber   Joseph Lynagh

**RECREATION LEAGUE**
Miss Helen Dickinson

**WELFARE SOCIETY**
Mrs. Ida Baxter

**MARGUERITE REBEKAH LODGE**
Mrs. E. E. Carpenter   Mrs. Floyd Thompson   Mrs. Chas. Wiggins

**DAUGHTERS OF LIBERTY**
Mrs. Wm. Mortimer   Mrs. Josiah Thompson   Mrs. Alfred Strickland

**HOLY NAME SOCIETY**
James McKelvey

**PROTECTION ENGINE COMPANY**
Eugene E. Carpenter   Wm. Larkin

**SHERIFF'S RESERVE**
Richard D. Linthicum

**KNIGHTS OF COLUMBUS**
John J. Kennedy

**CARPENTERS AND JOINERS OF AMERICA NO. 1152**
Philip Fitzsimmons   W. C. Cocks   Wm. Mortimer

## ROLL OF HONOR

GRECCO, JOSEPH
GAMBALE, PETRI
GUNN, HARTFORD
GRAY, FREEMAN
GRIFFIN, WALTER LEROY
GRECCO, RALPH
GIBSON, GEORGE
GREY, JOHN E.
GRAVEN, WILLIAM
GUGGENHEIM, HARRY
GROSS, ALBERT J.
GUNN, ALBERT E.
GALLAGHER, FRANCIS
GOULD, JOHN
GRIFFITH, ARTHUR
HAWKES, STANLEY
HAWKES, NELSON
HOTCHKISS J. MORGAN
HEIN, JOSEPH Jr.
HEGEMAN, JAMES F.
HENNESSY, GERALD
HELDRING, ALEX
HOROBIN, WALTER
HALL, H. CLINTON
HERBERT, JOHN H.
HARRISON, HAROLD
HOOPER, ERNEST
HULTS, GEORGE LEROY
HEGEMAN, PAUL
HEDGES, ELALAINE A.
HANKINS, ELLIS
IMPERIAL, LEPOLD
JONES, OTTO
JONES, ARTHUR C.
JANDORF, SIDNEY
JONES, CLIFFORD
JONES, WILLIAM
JONES, CHARLES E.
KAINS, STANLEY
KNAPP, WILLIAM L.
KEHOE, ANDREW F.
KERRIGAN, A. A.
KLECKOWSKI, ZYGMONT
KOONS, HERBERT L.
KEHOE, JOHN
KEHOE, ANDREW W.
KIRK, ROBERT J.
LENCHISKI, PAUL
LAWRENCE, F. S.
LYNCH, PETER
LONG, HARRY J.
LAIOLA, J. R.
LOTHIAN, ROBERT
LAWRENCE, BURCHARD R.
LONG, SETH
LOTHIAN, JOSEPH
LANCELLA, MICHAEL
LA PLACA, JOSEPH
LIOTTI, CHARLES
LASKIN, STEPHEN B.
LANDY, STEPHEN R.
LEWIS, CHARLES A.
LAWRENCE, WALLACE
MONGELLUZZO, ANGELO M.
MONZIGNE, AITOMO FRED
MESSENGER, ERNEST
METESWICH, PHILIP
MORGAN, WARREN
MONTROSS, WILLIAM B.
MARKLAND, BENJAMIN
MAHONEY, JAMES E.
MALCOLM, JUDSON
MATTHEWS, WILBUR
MARCIANO, RAFFAELI
MOSCHENROSS, MICHAEL
MULLON, WILBERT
MOSHIER, CLARENCE
MONGILLO, PASQUALE
MARINO, CHARLES
MITCHELL, EVERITT
MUZANTE, CHARLES
MACKEY, WALTER P.
MIGHETTI, GIOVANNI
MASI, JOSEPH
MILLER, GEORGE G.
MALONEY, MARTIN
MANSO, JOHN
McGIRR, TERRY
McCONNELL, TERRY
McKEE, RUSSELL
NORRIS, CHARLES G.
NEMBACH, ALBERT
NONBENCKI, JULIAN
NOVENSKI, TONY
NOLAN, THOMAS
NELSON, GOTTFRED
NEVILLE, ROBERT
NEMBACH, GEORGE
NEULIST, C. J. D.
NEVILLE, MICHAEL F.
NELSON, WALTER C.
OWENS, ARTHUR
O'SHAUGHNESSY, FRANK

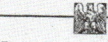

## ROLL OF HONOR

PERCIVAL, EDWARD
PETERSEN, SAMUEL
POULSON, THOMAS
POLLIZZI, FRANK
PASDERSKY, JOSEPH
PICATI, ALFONSO
PETERS, CLEMENT J.
PIERCE, ROLAND
PICARDI, ALESSANDRO
PICONE, JOSEPH
PALMER, JOSEPH
PEARCE, CLARENCE F.
POTTER, WILLIAM R.
PETERSEN, JOHN
PEDICINO, ALBERINO
POOL, CLYDE
PONIELLO, ANTONIO
PALMA, ALPHONSO
PARSONS, COL.
RIGNEY, MICHAEL
RUMENS, WILLIAM
ROMANO, TOMASSO
ROBERTSON, EARL
RAYNOR, WILLIAM
SLEE, JAMES
SOUSA, JOHN P.
SMITH, WALTER C.
SIZER, ROBERT
SIZER, THEODORE
SMITH, ROGER
SMITH, JOHN A.
SMITH, HARRY C.
SLOANE, BYRON
SMULL, THOMAS L.
SEAMAN, HAROLD
SEAMAN, SILAS
STANNARD, DANIEL B.
SMITH, EDWIN H.
SICCA, NICHOLA
STRICKLAND, GEORGE
SINGLETON, EDWARD
SEAMAN, CLARENCE
SMITH, FRANK B. Jr.
STANNARD, EDSON
SEIFTS, NELSON
SIMON, AUGUST A.
SMITH, HAROLD
SCHENCK, WILLIAM
STRICKLAND, EDWARD
SWANSON, ALFRED
STENBERG, JOHANNES
SCHAEFER, GUS.
SANTINELLO, SALVATORE
SHIELDS, JOHN J. F.
STRICKLAND, ARTHUR C.
SOLETO, AMELLE
SINGLETON, JOHN
SLOAN, CYRIL
THAYER, GEORGE A. 3rd.
TYSON, WILLIAM O.
TETA, FRANK
TETA, MICHAEL
TJARKS, EDWARD
THOMPSON, WILLIAM J.
TRUMAN, IRVING
THAYER, WILLIAM F.
TASSONI, BRUNO
TOWNSEND, RUBEN
TYLINSKI, WILLIAM
TYSON, DAVID L.
TETA, RAFELO
VERITY, ROBERT
VANDERWALL, CHARLES
VILLANI, VINCENZO
VICARELLI, ALFRED
VERNON, WILLIAM C.
VILLANI, JAMES
WILLIS, SAMUEL
WYSONG, DONALD D.
WILKINSON, SYLVENUS
WORTH, WILFRED
WILKINSON, SAMUEL, Jr.
WILCOX, ALLEN J.
WENNER, ARTHUR
WANSOR, CLARENCE
WIGGINS, ARTHUR
WHYTE, PATRICK
WALKER, REGINALD
WANSOR, DAVID
WANSER, ALFRED G.
WATTS, JESSE
WILLIAMS, DAVID, Jr.
YOUNG, ROY O.
YOUNG, RUSSELL
YOUNG, STANLEY

*Many other names have come to the notice of the committee, but we have been unable to locate or identify any of them, hence their absence from this list. The committee will be glad to receive any names that have been omitted if accompanied with sufficient information to warrant placing them on the honor roll.*

# From the Martin Cocks Collection

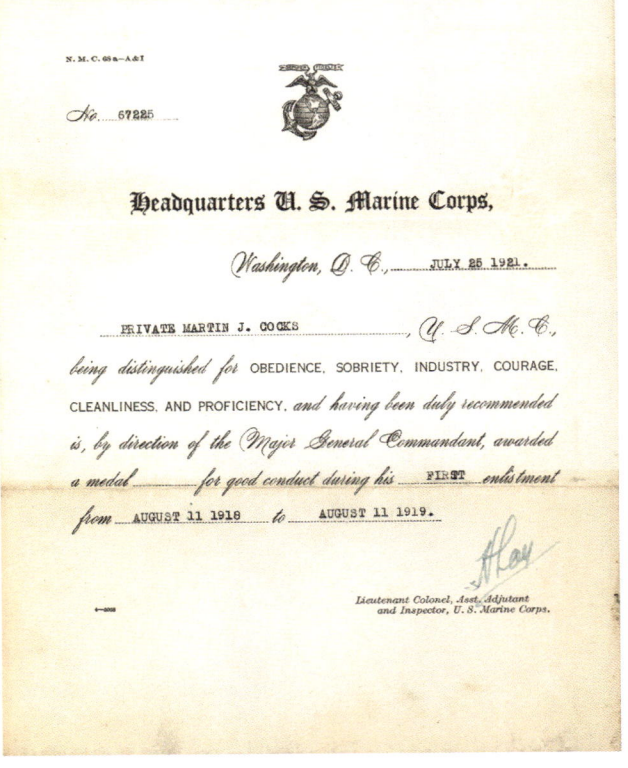

**Right:** War Service Certificate, United States Marine Corps, for honorable active service, at "Parris Island, S.C.; Quantico, Va.; 1st Regiment U.S. Marines, A.E.F. France; Hampton Roads, Va." .
—Donated by Janet Cocks Chudd

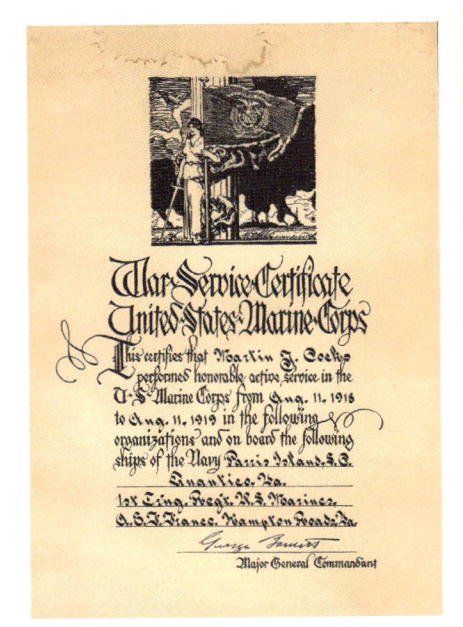

**Above:** 1921 Good Conduct Medal Certificate for Private Martin J. Cocks, distinguished for his obedience, sobriety, industry, courage, cleanliness, and proficiency, during his first enlistment from August 11, 1918 to August 11, 1919.
—Donated by Janet Cocks Chudd

**Martin Cocks' medals, left to right:**
1. Eagle and "United States Forces 1917-1918." Presented to local veterans from the people of Port Washington. Red, white, and blue ribbon.
2. Eagle on globe; reverse: Veterans of Foreign Wars." Red, white, yellow, and blue ribbon.
3. Dog tag, "Martin J. Cocks 8.11.18 USMC." Identification tags first issued in 1906. In 1916, two tags were issued. In the event of death, one to remain with the body and one for record keeping.
4. Angel of Victory; reverse: list of countries in "The Great War of Civilization," "France" in bar atop multi-colored ribbon.
5. Eagle on globe; reverse: Veterans of Foreign Wars." Red, white, yellow, and blue ribbon.
—Donated by Janet Cocks Chudd

120  WWI: The Homefront • Regiment • Cow Neck Peninsula Historical Society

**Above:** Port Washington Medal. Eagle and "1917-1918 United States Forces;" reverse: "Presented by the People of Port Washington to her Gallant Sons in Grateful Recognition of Patriotic Service in the World War 1917-1918." A red, white, and blue ribbon had been affixed to it.

**Above:** WWI New York State War Service Medal 1917-1919. Winged Victory and infantryman, ships in the background. Reverse has New York State coat-of-arms at top and "For Service 1917-1919 Presented by the State of New York" below. Banners on encircling wreath read "Belgium, Italy, Siberia" to left and "France, Germany, Russia" to right. Over 500,000 New Yorkers served and were eligible for the medal.

**Above:** Returning servicemen in front of Victoria Hotel at Main Street and Haven Avenue on Welcome Home Day. Each Port veteran was presented with a medal from the people of Port Washington, seen at top.

**Left:** WWI US Army Camp Souvenir. "American German War 1917" in center around infantryman and at bottom, "Declared April 6." The eagle with flags at the top is holding a banner that reads "Camp Souvenir" but the name of the camp was often inscribed in its place.

WWI: The Homefront • Regiment • Cow Neck Peninsula Historical Society **121**

## African Americans

One million African Americans registered for the draft. Over 350,000 served, most in segregated labor units for transport, building infrastructure, supply, and food industries. Port's **HOWARD DUMPSON** manned a guard house. There were no official segregation regulations, but note that the lower left corner of Mr. Dumpson's registration card was removed to indicate his African American status.

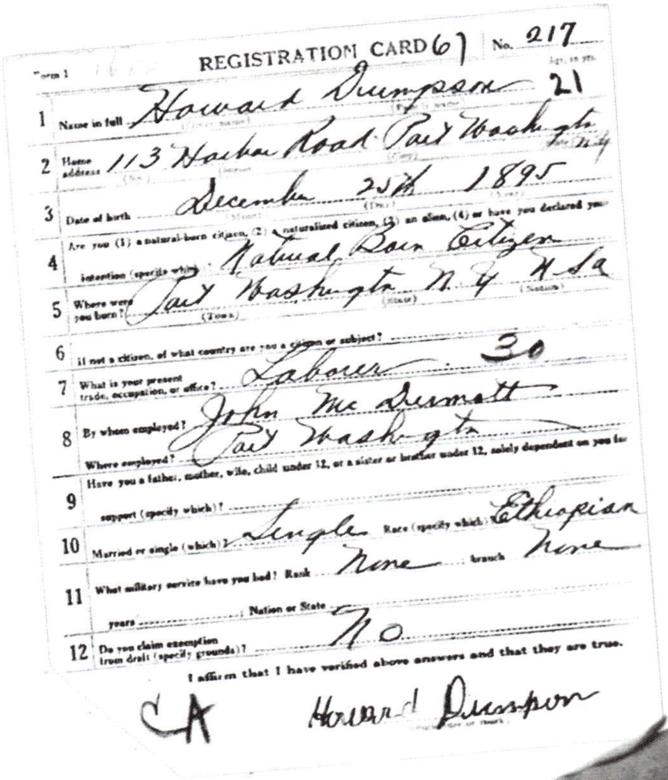

171 African Americans in New York's highly esteemed 369th Regiment, the "**HARLEM HELLFIGHTERS**," fought on the front line for 191 days. They were awarded the French Croix de Guerre, and **SGT. HENRY JOHNSON** was one of the first Americans to receive the French Croix de Guerre avec Palme, France's highest award for valor.

French Croix de Guerre avec Palme.

369th Regiment's Harlem Hellfighters marching up Fifth Avenue in the 1st Welcome Home Parade.

Sgt. Henry Johnson, "one of the five bravest American soldiers in the war."
— President Theodore Roosevelt

122  WWI: The Homefront • Regiment • Cow Neck Peninsula Historical Society

# The Elite

Elite young men, privileged by a background of wealth and influence, gained military officer status and garnered more opportunities in their lifetimes.

## THE GUGGENHEIM BROTHERS

Daniel Guggenheim, owner of Hempstead House, now in Sands Point Preserve, had two sons. In WWI the family was among the wealthiest in the world.

**Meyer Robert Guggenheim**
- Lt. Col.; Asst. Chief of Staff.
- U.S. Ambassador to Portugal.
- Director, Guggenheim Exploration Company.
- Interred, Arlington National Cemetery.

**Harry Frank Guggenheim**
- Lieutenant Commander.
- U.S. Ambassador to Cuba.
- He and 3rd wife founded Newsday; was President.
- Wedding gift: 90 acres of Sands Point property; built "Falaise."

Harry Frank Guggenheim entered service as Pilot, Lt. J.G.

## THE FIRST YALE UNIT

Twelve Yale University students aimed to fly for the war, so Trubee Davison founded a Yale Aero Club and Coastal Patrol Unit #1. In 1916 these students located a flying school in Port Washington with one Curtiss flying boat. Trubee's family supplied two more. They flew and maintained planes, living at the Davison estate, *Peacock Point*, in Lattingtown. The men became the first naval aviation unit, engaging enemy planes, chasing U-boats, and spotting enemy troops and munitions.

Float hangar, Manhasset Bay, north of Port Washington Yacht Club.

## Italian-Americans

Port Washington had Long Island's second largest community of Italian residents. Some returned to fight for their old country, as did Port's resident **JAMES VILLANI**. He was wounded twice, then returned from Italy to operate an inn.

**NICOLA SICA** worked in the sand pits, then as front line stretcher bearer in the 77th Division's Lost Battalion. A gas attack ruined his eyes, earning him a Purple Heart. Unable to return to work, he sold groceries from a horse and buggy. Each Armistice Day he had a party for 50-60 with fireworks and musicians on a flag-decorated truck. He was Grand Marshal at Memorial Day parades.

Cow Bay Inn, 402 Main Street, Port Washington, operated by James Villani.

---

Excerpts of letter to Mrs. William Mosher of 9 Ohio Ave. Reprinted in Port Washington News, December 20, 1918.

*My dear Mrs. Mosher:*

*in a few days your soldier will receive his honorable discharge and start for home...The Army has done everything it could to make him strong, fine, self-reliant, yet self-control[led]. It returns him to you a better man.*

*His fare and necessary expenses will be paid by the government. He may wear his uniform...for three months after date of discharge. The Government will also allow him to keep up, for the benefit of his family, his insurance at a very low rate he is now paying.*

*His return to civil life will bring new problems for you both to solve...Your Encouragement helped him while he was away, and in your hands and his rests the future of our country.*

*Sincerely yours,*
*C.GOUGER, 2nd Lieut., Camp Joseph E. Johnson, Jacksonville, Fla., Motor Transport Corps.*

## The Wounded

Returning soldiers included amputees and the disfigured, blind, and shell-shocked. Those disfigured had the greatest difficulty of all. The holes in their faces were sewn up, but there was no plastic surgery yet. The wounds were so horrific that many family members shunned their loved ones, and there were many suicides.

American sculptor **ANNA COLEMAN LADD** went to Paris' "Tin Noses Shop" where facial prostheses were made. She then led the American Red Cross Studio for Portrait Masks, designing and hand painting copper masks modeled on prewar photographs. Her creations changed lives.

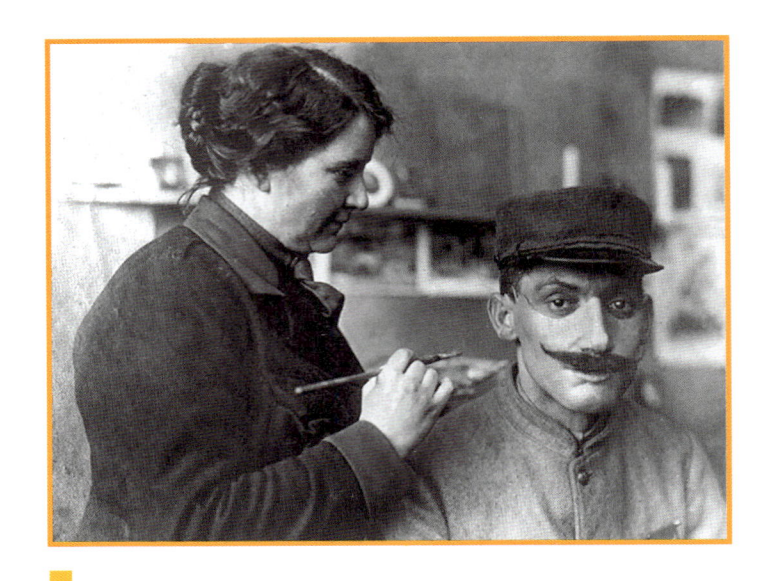

Anna Coleman Ladd creating a mask for a disfigured soldier.

## Quakers

Many of the old Cow Neck families were Quaker. They were drafted despite a firm belief in peace. Non-combative service was granted to some, whose war work included:

- Non-military jobs at camps, Red Cross;
- Humanitarian relief to civilians;
- Care for the wounded.

**THOMAS MOTT FRASER** was a Naval Reserve Boatswain's Mate, returning home to the family farm. He was the great-grandson of Martha and Edmund Willets, the first Willets family here at our Sands-Willets House.

Recruited Quakers included the **THAYER BROTHERS**.

**George Alexander Thayer III** was a private in the 19th Engineers Railway Regiment and acted as interpreter.

**William Frederick "Billy" Thayer** was in the Fifth Separate Battalion, U.S. Marines, in France where he was injured. See the excerpts from his letters home below.

---

"Last Letters from Billy: Mr. and Mrs. George A. Thayer Long For Some News from Their Wounded Son".
—Port Washington News, January 24, 1919

*Dearest Mother and Father:*

...We were sent right into the trenches, and went over the top in the third wave...We dug ourselves in up on a hill and here we were a fine target for the Boche guns...In one place, we had to lie down in shell holes, we were so mixed up there was a Blue Devil [elite French mountain infantry that wore blue cape and beret] in the same hole...The hole seemed small for two, but we got into it just as if we had been two brothers.

The fearful explosions when we are being shelled by "Fritz" are a great strain on one's nerves. There is always that feeling of whether you will get through or not... When you lie in a hole a couple of hours, with the big shells exploding around, then is when you do a lot of thinking. You do not want to, but you can't help it...I always think about the good old times we used to have in New Hampshire...I have been three days on one box of hard tack and one canteen of water; most of that went the first day...

The number of airplanes over here is huge...you cannot look up without seeing ten or twelve in the air...it gives you a funny feeling when you see one or the other come down in flames...A soldier is a pretty hard thing to kill, for all you hear. If I close my eyes I can see each foot of ground I have covered...and all the terrible sights that go with each foot.

Do not worry about me...my great love for you two, and yours for me, will carry me thru all dangers.

*Your own, Billy (Thayer)*

**The next letter from Billy, in Base Hospital, No. 27, Angers, France**

*Dearest Mother and Father:*

I have a bed, a nice, soft, bed with sheets and blankets and it seems as if I am in Heaven...I was wounded in the back by a piece of high explosive shell...The wound is not dangerous, only painful...a big, six inch shell exploded about ten feet away from us...I am worried about Scotty. I do not know whether he was wounded or not...I wish I knew where he was...I am a little tired now and weak, so I will close,

*Your own loving, Billy*

Note: On February 5, 1919, it was reported in the Brooklyn Times Union that Billy had recovered and was in Germany. Billy returned home after the war. He lived until age 73 and died in New Hampshire.

# Those We Lost

**In Flanders Fields**

In Flanders fields the poppies blow
Between the crosses, row on row,
    That mark our place; and in the sky
    The larks, still bravely singing, fly
Scarce heard amid the guns below.

We are the Dead. Short days ago
We lived, felt dawn, saw sunset glow,
    Loved and were loved, and now we lie
    In Flanders fields.

Take up our quarrel with the foe;
To you from failing hands we throw
    The torch; be yours to hold it high.
    If ye break faith with us who die
We shall not sleep, though poppies grow
    In Flanders fields.

—Lieutenant Colonel John McCrae

Somme American Cemetery, Bony, France. (Photo: American Battle Monuments Commission - ABMC.gov.)

## WWI American Cemeteries in Europe

There are many American cemeteries on foreign soil for the military casualties of the Great War. Some are small, in villages scattered throughout the countryside, often where the soldiers fell, and some are large and impressive.

Families could have their loved ones brought home for burial or have them buried in an overseas cemetery run by the United States. About 70% of the families chose to bring them home.

## Service Stars

The service flag was designed by a WWI Captain who had two sons on the front lines. The flags were to hang in a family's front window, with one blue star for each family member in the Armed Services. A blue star was covered with a gold star if a family member died in the line of duty.

This gentleman lost 11 children in the line of duty.

Banners carried in the 77th Division's May 6th parade bearing 2,356 Gold Stars in honor of those members who died.

WWI: The Homefront • Regiment • Cow Neck Peninsula Historical Society    **127**

# The Men of Port Washington Who Died

An attendee of Dartmouth, Lt. McCreery was a traveling salesman for the Chevrolet Motor Company. He enlisted April 10, 1917 at Mineola, sailing to France in December. One of the best American flight ferry pilots, he died in flight in a maneuvering accident. "He expected to be assigned to a new air squadron…for combat work at the front," said his father – New York Times, 6/1/1918. His family lived at 24 North Washington Street. The first Port soldier to die in WWI, a memorial to him is at the Band Shell.

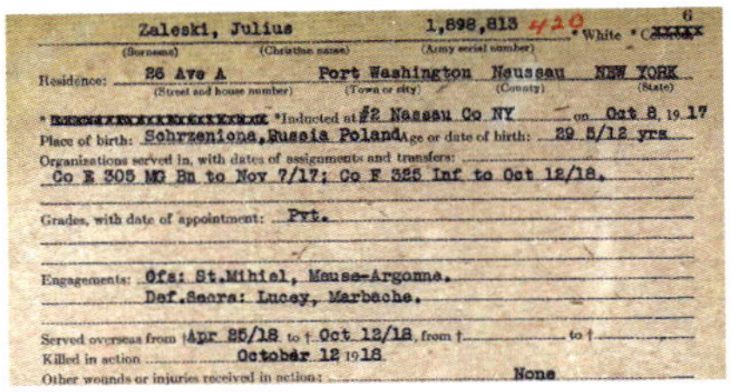

**Frank Plant McCreery**
1st Lieutenant, 19th Aero Squadron
5/28/1894 – 5/11/1918

**Julius Zaleski**
Private, 305th Machine Gun Battalion, 325th Infantry
c. 1888 – 10/12/1918

Private Zaleski, born in Schrzenicna, Russia-Poland, was inducted October 8, 1917 at age 29-1/2. He served in engagements at St. Mihiel, Meuse-Argonne, and Lucey and Marbache Sectors until being killed in action on October 12, 1918. He had lived at 26 Avenue A with his brother, Martin Zaleski.

Private Marino was inducted five weeks before graduating from Georgetown Law School. Engaged in battles for 200 days in the Meuse-Argonne and the Flanders Offensive, he died of pneumonia two days before Armistice. He was buried in Belgium, then interred in Westbury at Holy Rood. He had lived at 'Marino Castle' on Port Boulevard. Port's first Italian American to die in WWI, the Local Order Sons of Italy became the John Michael Marino Lodge; the VFW, the Henderson-Marino Post.

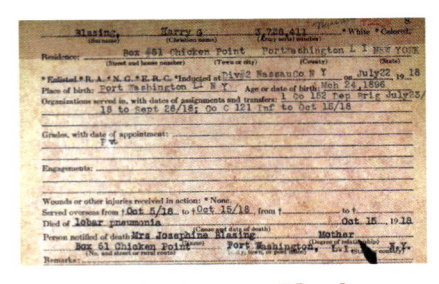

**John Michael Marino**
Private, 37th Division, National Guard
12/14/1894 – 11/9/1918

**Harry Gladstone Blasing**
Private, 152nd Depot Brigade, 121st Infantry
3/24/1896 – 10/15/1918

Private Blasing, inducted into the service on July 22, 1918, served until his death of lobar pneumonia three months later. He was born in Port Washington, was single, lived at 22 Valley Road, and was employed as a local gardener by Charles Fuller. His mother was Mrs. Josephine Blasing of Box 61, Chicken Point, in Port.

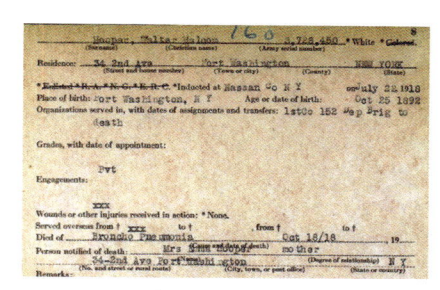

**Walter Malcolm Hooper**
Private, 1st Company, 152nd Depot Brigade
10/25/1892 – 10/18/1918

Private Hooper, inducted into the service on July 11, 1918, served until his death of bronco-pneumonia three months later. He was born in Port Washington, was single, and worked as a plumber for Clerke Heating and Plumbing Co. in town. He lived with his mother, Mrs. Emma Hooper, at 34 Second Avenue.

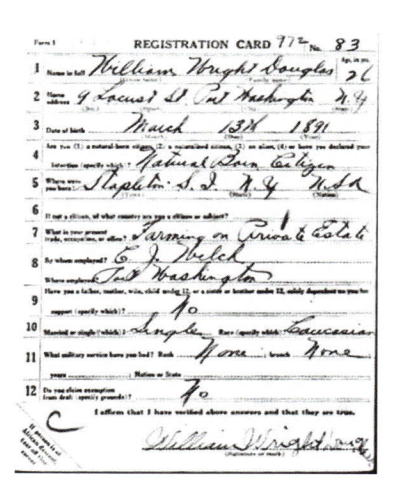

**William Wright Douglas**
Private, 310th Infantry, 78th Division
3/13/1891 – 2/12/1919

Private Douglas was wounded and then contracted lobar pneumonia. He was brought home and buried at Nassau Knolls Cemetery in Port by his father Cornelius and his younger brother Winfield. His mother, Mary, and five other siblings all lived at 9 Locust Street. He was single and had farmed on C.J. Welch's estate.

**William Edward Henderson**
Private, 77th Division, 307th Infantry
6/28/1895 – 9/14/1918

Private Henderson served as an orderly for Lt. Earl Felter (below) and survived 150 days of combat until September 2, 1918, when he went missing. Listed as MIA in November, only in May 1919 did Mr. and Mrs. William Henderson learn that their son had been killed in action in France along the Vesle River. He had lived at home at 26 Avenue B and is said to have cared for the Belmonts' horses in Sands Point. Port's VFW named their lodge the Henderson-Marino Post in his memory.

**Earle Barton Felter**
1st Lt., 77th Division, 307th Infantry
1893 – 9/14/1918

Lt. Felter was a summer resident of Port Washington. He was killed in action in the Argonne Forest along with his orderly, Port resident William E. Henderson (above). Lt. Felter was first memorialized in France, in the Oise-Aisne American Cemetery and was later interred at Green-Wood Cemetery in Brooklyn. His obituary appeared in The New York Times on Sunday, November 17, 1918, "the beloved son of Mr. and Mrs. George W. Felter, 522 Putnam Avenue, Brooklyn."

**We lost:**
- 4 men to pneumonia, likely influenza.
- 3 men killed in action.
- 1 man in a training exercise.

## Memorials

Throughout the nation, monuments were erected to honor those who served and those who gave their lives in World War 1. Our area was no exception.

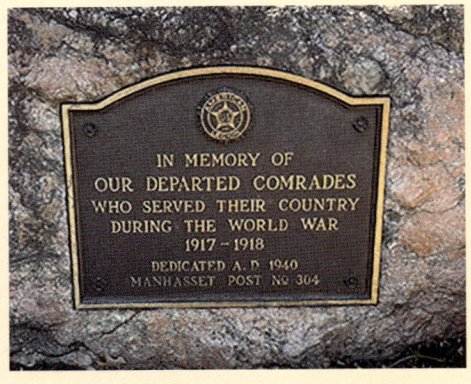

**Left:** Port Washington, Sunset Park
**Right, top:** Manhasset, Train Station
**Right, bottom:** Roslyn, Clock Tower

The Port Washington News 1921 Almanac. The poppy was selected as the memorial flower of American soldiers we lost in France, as immortalized in the poem, "In Flanders Fields." The American Legion urged everyone to wear the poppy on Memorial Day.

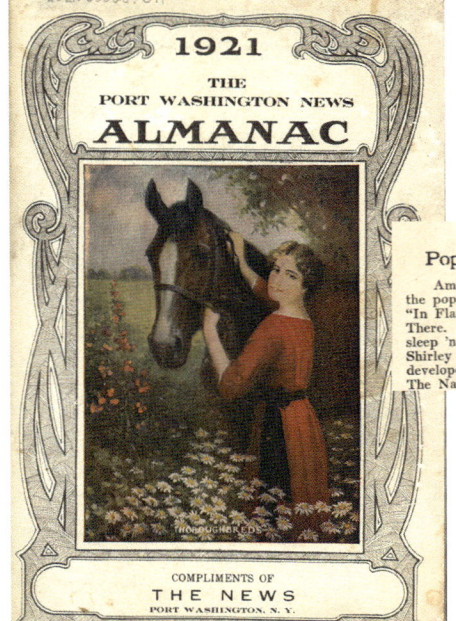

This Peace Dollar coin, newly minted in 1921, won a coin design competition portraying peace. The eagle rests on a mountaintop inscribed with the word "Peace" and holds an olive branch.

130   WWI: The Homefront • Regiment • Cow Neck Peninsula Historical Society

# Following the War, Visits to Sites Became Popular

Following the Great War, pilgrimages to battlefields became common for loved ones, veterans, and the merely curious. Family members were given an opportunity to visit the grave of their loved one, and veterans were able to pay their respects to their brothers-in-arms.

Guidebooks were printed with site information and itineraries. These trips continue, and to this day in Ypres, at 8:00 pm, traffic stops as buglers play "The Last Post" beneath the memorial arch.

The Centenary of WWI and a growing interest in genealogy has caused an increase in tourism to war museums, military hospitals, memorials and cemeteries, and battlefields and trails on the Western Front.

"Michelin Illustrated Guides to the Battlefields (1914-1918)" for "Verdun and the Battles for its Possession," and "Ypres and the Battles of Ypres." The interior photos in Ypres show two sites, before (top) and after (below) bombing

French postcard image of Lieutenant Quentin Roosevelt's tomb where he died in 1918 combat in Chamery, France.
— Postcard from the Collection of Fred Blumlein

# The Price of Freedom: An Army of Animals

From elephants to glow worms, no creature was too large or small to be harnessed by the peoples of the world for war. Countless millions of animals were put into service, without a choice, many performing heroically, and many suffering harrowing deaths for their efforts.

## General Animal Category

Animals' war roles were multi-purposed. Some served in the cavalry; some delivered messages on foot or in flight; some warned of gas attacks. Some did heavy labor hauling big loads, some attacked like soldiers; and some, if not most, served as morale boosters, providing affection to men far from home under grim conditions. Some were simply mascots enjoyed by the men: bear cubs, foxes, crows, raccoons, monkeys, lion cubs, baby alligators, and, of course, all the more standard animal friends.

**Elephants, Buffalo, Oxen:** These beasts of burden plodded through all weather, delivering munitions and supplies and hauling away obstacles in their paths.

**Camels** required little food or water in arid terrain. They carried men, supplies, or the deceased. Their irritability kept them apart from other animals.

**Cats** kept the trenches free of rodents and ran off at the first sign of gas, warning the men. They also provided much needed comfort to the men.

**Canaries** smelling gas before the soldiers did made a clamor and flew away, alerting soldiers to don their masks.

**Baboons:** A mascot turned soldier, Cpl. Jackie's sensitive smell and hearing made him an excellent sentry.

**Glow Worms** in jars provided non-flickering light to soldiers reading maps and reports in dark trenches.

**Slugs** closed their breathing pores and compressed their bodies on detecting gas, alerting soldiers to mask up.

## Horses, Donkeys, and Mules

Eight million horses and innumerable mules and donkeys perished. They died of shellfire, starvation, thirst, exposure to the elements, exhaustion, disease, and drowning in mud. They exhibited bravery and unusual stamina, transporting ammunition, supplies, and men through the muck and horrors of war.

**Top:** Work horses straining up a hill with an overladen wagon.

**Second:** A horse stuck in the mud was a common sight. They often could not be freed.

**Third:** U.S. horses were sent by train to the East Coast ports and shipped overseas.

**Overlay:** Gas mask with built-in goggles custom made for a horse.

**Papier-Maché Horses** were crafted for surveillance. Under cover of night, a dead horse would be dragged off and replaced by a fake horse a soldier could crawl into.

## Dogs

Dogs delivered messages and supplies, laid wire, detected mines, located wounded, patrolled their areas, served through deplorable conditions, and persevered even when wounded. Their courage and loyalty was unending, and the devotion between dog and handler was profound.

**Cigarette dog:** All soldiers had to get to soldiers

**Dogs on the front line**
**Top, left:** Two Red Cross dogs bringing medical supplies to front.
**Top, right:** Dog wearing custom gas mask with built-in goggles.
**Above, left:** Dog running telephone wire to the front line.
**Above, right:** Dog kennel in France.

**"Lynbrook Dog Won** Don served in the 106 mascot. His company two gold wound strip to his leg and shrapne

### Sergeant Stubby – Stray, Stowaway, Soldier

When Stubby was discovered aboard ship, he raised his paw, saluting as taught, sealing his fate as mascot. But he became far more in 1½ years of 4 major offensives and 17 battles. He howled in fright, yet located wounded soldiers in No Man's Land and ran to get help. One night he sneaked out of the trench and took a German prisoner by clamping down on his pants until help came.

SERGEANT STUBBY HERO DOG OF WWI A BRAVE STRAY

**Stubby's Mask** made after he was mustard gassed. He later saved an entire company, alerting them to incoming gas.

WWI: The Homefront • Regiment • COW NECK PENINSULA HISTORICAL SOCIETY • www.cowneck.org

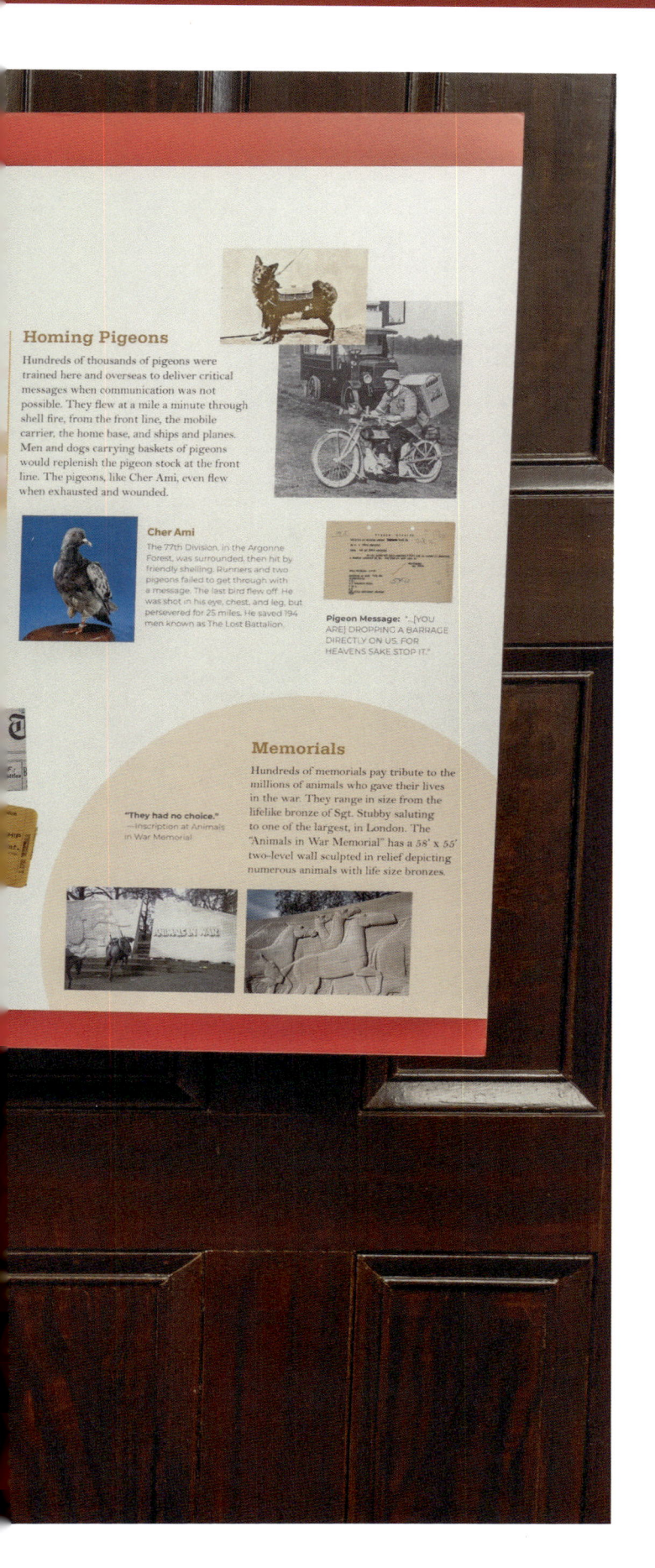

## THE PRICE OF FREEDOM:
# An Army of Animals

From elephants to glow worms, no creature was too large or small to be harnessed by the peoples of the world for war. Countless millions of animals were put into service, without a choice, many performing heroically and many suffering harrowing deaths for their efforts.

WWI: The Homefront • Regiment • Cow Neck Peninsula Historical Society

# General Animal Category

Animals' war roles were multi-purposed. Some served in the cavalry; some delivered messages on foot or in flight; some warned of gas attacks. Some did heavy labor hauling big loads; some attacked like soldiers; and some, if not most, served as morale boosters, providing affection to men far from home under grim conditions. Some were simply mascots enjoyed by the men: bear cubs, foxes, crows, raccoons, monkeys, lion cubs, baby alligators, and, of course, all the more standard animal friends.

**Cats** kept the trenches free of rodents and ran off at the first sign of gas, warning the men. They also provided much needed comfort to the men.

**Canaries** smelling gas before the soldiers did made a clamor and flew away, alerting soldiers to don their masks.

**Glow Worms** in jars provided non-flickering light to soldiers reading maps and reports in dark trenches. (Photo: Wikipedia)

**Slugs** closed their breathing pores and compressed their bodies on detecting gas, alerting soldiers to mask up.

**Elephants, Buffalo, Oxen:** These beasts of burden plodded through all weather, delivering munitions and supplies and hauling away obstacles in their paths.

**Camels** required little food or water in arid terrain. They carried men, supplies, or the deceased. Their irritability kept them apart from other animals.

**Baboons:** A mascot turned soldier, Cpl. Jackie's sensitive smell and hearing made him an excellent sentry.

## Horses, Donkeys, and Mules

Eight million horses and innumerable mules and donkeys perished. They died of shellfire, starvation, thirst, exposure to the elements, exhaustion, disease, and drowning in mud. They exhibited bravery and unusual stamina, transporting ammunition, supplies, and men through the muck and horrors of war.

▪ Gas mask with built-in goggles custom made for a horse.

▪ Work horses straining up a hill with an overladen wagon.

▪ A horse stuck in the mud was a common sight. They often could not be freed.

▪ U.S. horses were sent by train to the East Coast ports and shipped overseas.

▪ Papier-maché horses were crafted for surveillance. Under cover of night, a dead horse would be dragged off and replaced by a fake horse a soldier could crawl into.

WWI: The Homefront • Regiment • Cow Neck Peninsula Historical Society

## Dogs

Dogs delivered messages and supplies, laid wire, detected mines, located wounded, patrolled their areas, served through deplorable conditions, and persevered even when wounded. Their courage and loyalty was unending, and the devotion between dog and handler was profound.

### Dogs on the front line

**Top, left:** Two Red Cross dogs bringing medical supplies to front.
**Bottom, left:** Dog kennel in France.

**Top, right:** Dog wearing custom gas mask with built-in goggles.
**Bottom, right:** Dog running telephone wire to the front line.

Cigarette dog: All sorts of supplies had to get to soldiers at the front.

**"Lynbrook Dog Won Fame in Army"**
Don served in the 106th Infantry as mascot. His company blanket bore two gold wound stripes for the bullet to his leg and shrapnel to his neck.

136  WWI: The Homefront • Regiment • Cow Neck Peninsula Historical Society

'SERGEANT STUBBY
HERO DOG OF WWI
A BRAVE STRAY'

New York T

NEW YORK, THURSDAY, JULY 7, 1921.

Pershing Honors Stubby, Mascot of A. E. F.;
Pins Medal on Dog Hero of 17 Battles

### Sergeant Stubby–Stray, Stowaway, Soldier

A stray puppy joined soldiers drilling on a Yale field. When it came time to ship overseas, Stubby silently hid under Private Conroy's greatcoat as they boarded. Stubby, once discovered by the commanding officer, raised his paw, saluting as taught, sealing his fate as mascot. But he became far more in 1½ years of 4 major offensives and 17 battles. He howled in fright, yet located wounded soldiers in No Man's Land and ran to get help. One night he sneaked out of the trench and took a German prisoner by biting him and clamping down on his pants until help came.

**Middle, clockwise from left:** Stubby in coat made for him by French women, covered by his medals.

Post-war, Stubby led parades and appeared on floats.

Stubby's custom mask made after he was gassed, which taught him to alert men to the onset of fumes.

**Right:** Susan Bahary's life-size bronze sculpture, "Stubby Salutes." On display at Trees of Honor Veterans' Park, CT and AKC Museum of the Dog, New York City. (Photo: Jay Daniel)

WWI: The Homefront • Regiment • Cow Neck Peninsula Historical Society **137**

## Homing Pigeons

Hundreds of thousands of pigeons were trained here and overseas to deliver critical messages when other communication was not possible. They flew at a mile a minute through shell fire, from the front line, the mobile carrier, the home base, and ships and planes. Men and dogs carrying baskets of pigeons would replenish the pigeon stock at the front line. Pigeons like Cher Ami, flew even when exhausted and wounded.

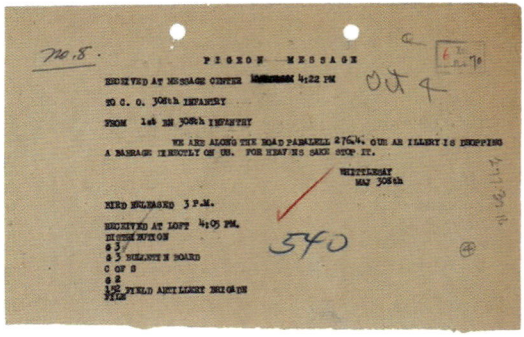

**Pigeon Message:** "…[YOU ARE] DROPPING A BARRAGE DIRECTLY ON US. FOR HEAVENS SAKE STOP IT."

## Cher Ami

The 77th Division, in the Argonne Forest, was surrounded, then hit by friendly shelling. Runners and two pigeons failed to get through with a message. The last bird flew off. He was shot in his eye, chest, and leg, but persevered for 25 miles. He saved 194 men known as The Lost Battalion.

**Cher Ami**
(Photo: Division of Political and Military History, National Museum of American History, Smithsonian Institution)

**"They had no choice."**
—Inscription at Animals in War Memorial

## Memorials

Hundreds of memorials pay tribute to the millions of animals who gave their lives in the war. They range in size from the lifelike bronze of Sgt. Stubby saluting to one of the largest, in London. The "Animals in War Memorial" has a 58' x 55' two-level wall sculpted in relief depicting numerous animals with life size bronzes marching through it.

Two weary mules of bronze plod towards the wall, a symbol of the war. Through the wall on the upper level, a bronze horse and dog in colorful gardens represent hope.
(Photo: The Animals in War Memorial, animalsinwar.org.uk)

The longer section of the wall has bas-relief sculpture of the numerous animals lost in conflicts.
(Photo: The Animals in War Memorial, animalsinwar.org.uk)

140  WWI: The Homefront • Suffragettes • Cow Neck Peninsula Historical Society

# Suffragettes

"On Saturday Gen'l Rosalie Jones thundered at our gates, and they were thrown open to her at the first assault by friendly hands. Our Mayor (if we had one) would have presented to her the keys of the city, if we had a key."

—**Port Washington News, August 9, 1913**

# Women of Protest

Women suffrage organizations had differing viewpoints during the war years on how to achieve the right to vote. NAWSA suffragists felt their great contributions to the war effort would suffice. NWP activist suffragettes led by Lucy Burns and Alice Paul strongly disagreed, believing that more assertive means were needed. They received brutal mistreatment for their efforts.

**NAWSA:** National American Woman Suffrage Association
**NWP:** National Woman's Party

**March 3, 1913:**

## Woman Suffrage Procession

Up to 10,000 suffragists from all over the country marched down Pennsylvania Avenue as 500,000 gathered for President Wilson's inauguration the next day, totally overshadowing his arrival by train. The parade, complete with floats and bands, organized by Lucy Burns and Alice Paul, protested the exclusion of women from the political culture. A hostile mob blocked their way, becoming violent. They assaulted and taunted the women, spitting, slapping, and burning them with their cigars, as they screamed and cursed them. The oppositionists were regarded poorly, fostering the suffragists' cause and launching a police investigation.

**January 10, 1917:**

## "Silent Sentinels"

Six days a week for over 2½ years, 2000 women silently picketed the White House, its first picketing ever, letting their placards and banners speak for them. Organized by Alice Paul of the NWP, they continued with their goals for national woman suffrage during the war years, differing from other suffrage groups. This constant reminder to President Wilson of national suffrage was initially tolerated, but then the suffragettes were harassed, assaulted, arrested, and jailed for "obstructing traffic." Supporters brought them hot bricks to stand on and warm drinks, but many anti-suffragists pushed and heckled them and destroyed their banners. And yet these peaceful demonstrators returned, with new banners, day after day, for close to three years.

**November 14, 1917:**
## "Night of Terror"

The Silent Sentinels jailed in the Occaquan Workhouse suffered intolerable conditions with fetid water, filthy bedding, and worm-ridden rancid food, housed with syphilitic women with open sores. In response to their hunger strikes, they were force-fed fluids and raw eggs through tubes shoved down their throats.

The brutal abuse culminated on a November night when the prison guards let loose. They dragged 33 women to the men's cells, locking some in with prisoners having delirium tremens. They handcuffed and manacled them, threatened them with straitjackets and mouth braces, beat them and terrorized them, and left them to lie there or shackled to the bars, barely conscious.

When the Silent Sentinels were asked why they continued in their efforts in light of the danger, they replied that it was to ensure no other women would have to endure their suffering.

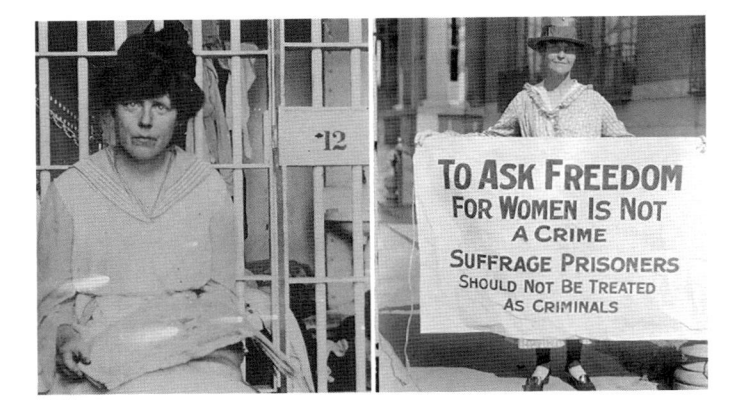

**August 18, 1920:**
## The 19th Amendment of the Constitution of the United States

President Wilson finally supported a national suffrage amendment in January 1918, following the Night of Terror. The House of Representatives approved the amendment, with the Senate following over a year later. Next, on to the states for ratification, and both major suffrage groups, NAWSA and NWP, worked unflaggingly to gain the support of 36 of the 48 states. It finally came down to one vote, and an anti-suffragist representative from Tennessee bowed to his mother's pressure and supported the measure. It is said he had to take cover in the State Capitol.

> "The right of citizens of the United States to vote shall not be denied or abridged by the United States or by any State on account of sex.
> 
> Congress shall have power to enforce this article by appropriate legislation."

In 1875, Susan B. Anthony and Elizabeth Cady Stanton wrote these words that were presented to Congress in 1878 and every year thereafter. It took 41 years for them to be approved by Congress.

# Woman Suffrage Timeline

Local suffrage activities are presented in a select framework of both New York State and National suffrage events. The suffragist's pursuits led to the landmark vote for woman suffrage in New York State in 1917. The final milestone achievement was reached in 1920 with the ratification of the 19th Amendment, granting women in all 48 states the right to vote.

Headquarters of the National Association Opposed to Woman Suffrage in New York City, founded 1911.

New York City Women's March, October 23, 1915.

## UP TO 1850s

### NATIONAL

**1756:** Lydia Chapin Taft votes in town meetings in MA, first woman to vote legally in Colonial America.

**1776:** Property-owning women get right to vote in NJ, but married women cannot own property.

**1837:** 1st National Female Anti-Slavery Convention in NYC attended by 81 delegates from 12 states.

### NEW YORK

**1848:** Tea party at activist Jane Hunt's is catalyst for 1st women's rights convention at Seneca Falls, 6 days later.

**1848:** Seneca Falls Convention with 300 attending. Elizabeth Cady Stanton presents new women's rights manifesto, the Declaration of Sentiments.

**1848:** NY's Married Woman's Property Act, but married women can't enter contracts, so suffragists do not wed.

### LOCAL

**1848:** Lucretia Mott, a leader at Seneca Falls Convention, has Cow Neck husband James Mott as key speaker.

James Mott and Lucretia Mott

## THE 1850s

### NATIONAL

**1850:** 1st National Women's Rights Convention in MA. 1,000 delegates/11 states. Event scorned by reporters.

**1851:** Abolitionist Sojourner Truth delivers speech, dubbed racially as *"Ain't I a Woman?"* in OH. Born into slavery in NY, she spoke with no southern idiom.

**1853:** 1st Feminist newspaper, *The Una*, in RI.

### NEW YORK

**1850:** 6,000 signatures on petition for women's rights have little effect on legislature.

**1851:** Susan B. Anthony and Elizabeth Cady Stanton first meet in Seneca Falls.

## THE 1860s

### NATIONAL

**1861-1865:** Civil War. Suffragists focus on abolishing slavery instead of the right to vote.

**1868:** *The Revolution* published. "Men, their rights and nothing more; women, their rights and nothing less!"

**1868:** U.S. suffrage amendment first brought to Congress.

**1869:** Boston's **AWSA** formed for state suffrage.

### NEW YORK

**1866:** E.C. Stanton runs for Congress in NY's 8th District. Women can't vote; can run for office. She receives 24 votes.

**1869:** E.C. Stanton & Susan B. Anthony found NY's **NWSA**, for constitutional amendment, more rights.

**1869:** 15th Amendment guarantees all men right to vote. NWSA wants 16th Amendment for all suffrage. Frederick Douglass breaks from group.

Elizabeth Cady Stanton and Susan B. Anthony

## THE 1870s

### NATIONAL

**1870:** Male-dominated Wyoming's women first to win vote.

**1871:** Anti-Suffrage Party founded by Civil War generals' wives.

**1874:** Women's Christian Temperance Union supports prohibition and suffragists, so liquor lobbyists fear both.

**1878:** Woman Suffrage Amendment proposed to Congress using exact wording of 19th Amendment.

### NEW YORK

**1873:** Susan B. Anthony and 15 women illegally vote for Ulysses S. Grant in 1872. Anthony convicted and fined.

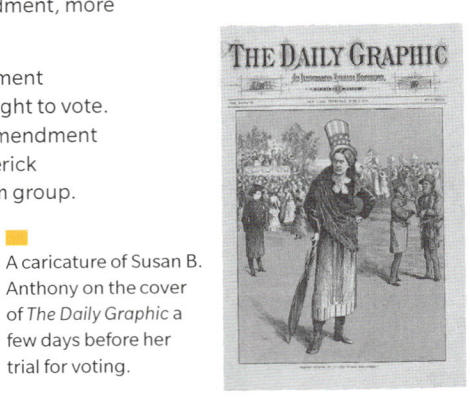

A caricature of Susan B. Anthony on the cover of *The Daily Graphic* a few days before her trial for voting.

---

**AWSA:** American Woman Suffrage Association
**NAWSA:** National American Woman Suffrage Association
**NWSA:** National Woman Suffrage Association

*Suffragists parade down Fifth Avenue, 1917.*

*Mrs. Alice Burke and Mrs. Nell Richardson in the suffrage automobile "Golden Flyer" to drive from New York to San Francisco, April 7, 1916.*

## THE 1880s

### NATIONAL

**1887:** Senate defeats 1st vote on woman suffrage, 34 to 16, with 25 absent.

*Suffragists in parade, ca. 1910 – 1915.*

## THE 1890s

### NATIONAL

**1890: NAWSA** formed, combining NWSA and AWSA, with Carrie Chapman Catt as leader.

**1895:** E.C. Stanton publishes *The Woman's Bible.*

**1890s:** Women's ballot boxes employed to ensure women voting only for municipal portions of ballot.

**1896:** Mary C. Terrell, Ida B. Wells, Harriet Tubman form National Association of Colored Women.

### NEW YORK

**1894:** 600,000 signatures on suffrage petition presented to NYS Constitutional Convention, to no avail.

### LOCAL

**1895:** Mariana Wright Chapman forms Political Equality League, hosting suffrage meetings at her Sands Point home, Heronwood.

## THE 1900s

### NATIONAL

**1909:** Alva Vanderbilt Belmont founds Political Equality Assoc. under NAWSA, funds NAWSA's move from OH to NYC.

### NEW YORK

**1903:** Women's Trade Union League of NY formed for working women to unionize and vote.

**1907:** NYC's 1st Unofficial Woman Suffrage March; 23 participants. Marches continued and grew.

**1909:** At Carnegie Hall, Carrie Chapman Catt founds Woman Suffrage Party of Greater New York.

### LOCAL

**1901:** Anna and Lila Willets attend convention of National Association for Woman Suffrage in Minneapolis.

**1902:** Queens and Nassau County's 6th Annual Convention of the Political Equality League (PEL); Mariana Wright Chapman and Anna Willets, speakers.

**1904:** Local women go to D.C.'s Political Equality League (PEL): Mrs. Chapman, Mrs. Mott, Mrs. Nostrand, Miss Willets.

## THE 1910s

### NATIONAL

**1910:** Suffragists parade in 50 autos, deliver 404,000 signatures for federal suffrage to Congress.

**1911:** Mrs. A. Dodge opposes Suffrage with women of power, clergy, brewers, Southerners.

**1912:** Theodore Roosevelt's Bull Moose Party supports suffrage.

### NEW YORK

**1910:** 1st NYC Suffrage Parade.

**1911:** 3,000 supporters march in 2nd Suffrage Parade in NYC. 70,000 watch.

**1912:** 20,000 supporters march in 3rd Suffrage Parade in NYC. 500,000 watch.

**1912:** Rosalie Gardiner Jones leads 140-mile march from Bronx to Albany, asks governor to endorse suffrage amendment.

### LOCAL

**1910:** Alva Belmont forms PEL Woman Physicians & Surgeons with 12 female doctors.

**1911:** 18,000 to Mineola Fair. Mrs. Belmont hosts meeting. "One lone man present."

**1912:** "Whirlwind Campaign" in suffrage-bannered car tours L.I.

**1912:** Property-owning women vote on roads.

**1912:** Mrs. Belmont opens Suffrage Cafeteria on E. 41st St., 1 of her 11 "Votes for Women" establishments in city and L.I.

WWI: The Homefront • Suffragettes • Cow Neck Peninsula Historical Society

*"General" Rosalie Jones and Port Washington suffragists join Fireman's Parade, marching past what is now Finn MacCool's Restaurant.*

*Suffragists picketing the White House in 1917.*

## 1913

### NATIONAL

**1913:** Rosalie Jones, Votes for Women Pilgrimage, 295-mile protest hike, NY to DC, during Wilson's election.

**1913:** 8,000 suffragists parade in DC with 500,000 onlookers who engage in violent protest and abuse.

**1913:** Alice Paul and Lucy Burns organize Congressional Union, later named National Woman's Party (NWP).

### NEW YORK

**1913:** NY State Legislature approves bill for statewide referendum on women's suffrage.

**1913:** Inspired by Pilgrimage to DC, 10,000+ women and men march on NYC's Fifth Avenue for suffrage.

### LOCAL

**1913:** All-night promotional "Aerial Party" on Hempstead Plains aviation field attended by 200.

**1913:** "General" Rosalie Jones addresses Port's suffrage meeting, and they impulsively join the Fireman's Parade.

**1913:** Horse carriage "Spirit of 1776" donated for parades.

**1913:** Port H.S. mass meeting. Mrs. Brown spoke about "Taxation without Representation is Tyranny."

## 1914—1915

### NATIONAL

**1914:** Mrs. Frank Leslie, publisher of *Leslie's Weekly*, donates $1 million to Carrie Chapman Catt for the cause.

**1915:** S.B. Field leads 3-month auto tour, California to DC, gathering 500,000 signatures petitioning Congress.

### NEW YORK

**1915:** NYC suffrage parade of 40,000, largest ever.

**1915:** Ida Bunce Sammis organizes pilgrimages across LI: North and South Forks, Hempstead, Glen Cove.

**1915:** NY voters reject referendum.

### LOCAL

**1914:** Port's Equal Suffrage League sets up in Main Street's Davis Building with women's baking exchange.

**1915:** Suffragists traverse L.I. demonstrating canning food, to be "the best sort of woman in the home."

**1915:** Port's women go to polls wearing suffrage badges to encourage all to vote for upcoming amendment.

**1915:** Suffragists at Mineola Fair with sample voting paraphernalia: polling booths, boxes, registrations.

## 1916

### NATIONAL

**1916:** Jeannette Rankin first woman elected to U.S. Congress.

**1916:** Suffragists fly over President Wilson's yacht and drop suffrage petitions.

**1916:** Woodrow Wilson announces the Democratic Party supports suffrage.

*Suffrage parade following President Wilson's 1916 support of suffrage.*

### LOCAL

**1916:** Nassau County Suffrage Convention elects Mrs. Grace Greene of Sands Point as chairwoman.

**1916:** Mineola Fair's suffrage booth had information bureau and "Rest for the Weary" area with nurse.

**1916:** Mrs. Laidlaw joined Mrs. Greene in roadster to tour 20 towns, speaking and picnicking on the way.

## 1917

### NATIONAL

**1917:** NWP silently pickets the White House. These "Silent Sentinels" ultimately incarcerated and abused.

**1917:** NWP leader Alice Paul put in solitary in prison's mental ward.

**1917:** In response to public outcry and inability to stop hunger strikes, a number of picketers released from jail.

### NEW YORK

**1917:** Women, military families, workers, professionals, march in Women's Parade of 20,000 on 5th Avenue to link suffrage to war effort.

**1917:** Linking suffrage with American values allows NY suffrage referendum to pass. NY women have the vote.

**1917:** Alva V. Belmont hosts thousands at Belasco Theatre, NYC, honoring newly released White House picketers from jail.

### LOCAL

**1917:** Suffragists take military census of Nassau County males over 16, due to organizational framework.

**1917:** Local suffragists urge husbands to join Home Defense Corps. to support war effort.

**1917:** Theodore Roosevelt and Mrs. Laidlaw open 2nd NYS suffrage campaign with 500 at Sagamore Hill.

WWI: The Homefront • Suffragettes • Cow Neck Peninsula Historical Society

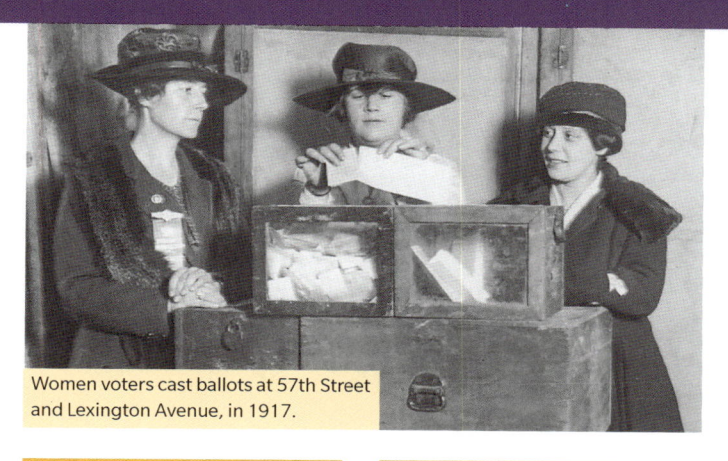

Women voters cast ballots at 57th Street and Lexington Avenue, in 1917.

Women's Party headquarters after sewing on the 36th star, celebrating the ratification of the 19th Amendment by Tennessee.

## 1918

### NATIONAL

**1918:** Woodrow Wilson endorses federal suffrage amendment on January 9.

**1918:** Rep. Jeanne Rankin debates suffrage in House. Passes by 1 vote, but the Senate won't vote on the bill.

**1918:** Wilson addresses Senate to support suffrage. Senate defeats bill: should be states' rights, not federal.

## 1919

### NATIONAL

**1919:** Suffragists heighten protests, burning Wilson in effigy, burning his hypocritical words.

**1919:** Formerly jailed suffragists cross the country on railroad car telling of their abuse.

**1919:** States with presidential suffrage climb to 15. House passes federal amendment, 304 to 89, then Senate, 56 to 25.

## 1920

### NATIONAL

**1920:** By June, 35 states of needed 36 of 48 ratify bill. Next was Tennessee's vote; suffragist supporters stalked, sent hate mail. 1st term legislator votes "aye" and seals the deal.

**1920:** The 19th Amendment is law. Women can now legally vote in all 48 states. Voter suppression still reigns, particularly in south.

**1920:** National American Woman Suffrage Association becomes start of the League of Women Voters.

### LOCAL

**1920:** National Woman's Party Conference at Beacon Towers, Sands Point.

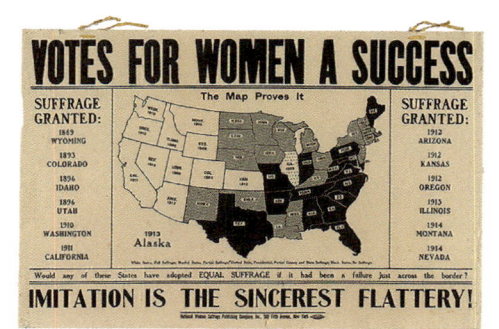

"Votes for Women a Success," showing first 13 states to give women the right to vote, ca. 1914.

League of Women Voters, first formed as a NAWSA committee, urged women to register to vote in their first election all over the country.

### LOCAL

**1918:** Alva V. Belmont hosts fundraisers, meetings, funds pickets, petitions, and prods Congress at her new Beacon Towers on tip of Sands Point.

**1918:** Cold Spring Harbor's Ida B. Sammis 1st woman in NYS Assembly, winning by 900 votes.

### LOCAL

**1919:** "Presidential Vote Aim for All Women" meeting at Beacon Towers.

*The Suffragist* "At Last," June 21, 1919 issue, after the 19th Amendment was passed by Congress on June 4, 1919.

WWI: The Homefront • Suffragettes • Cow Neck Peninsula Historical Society

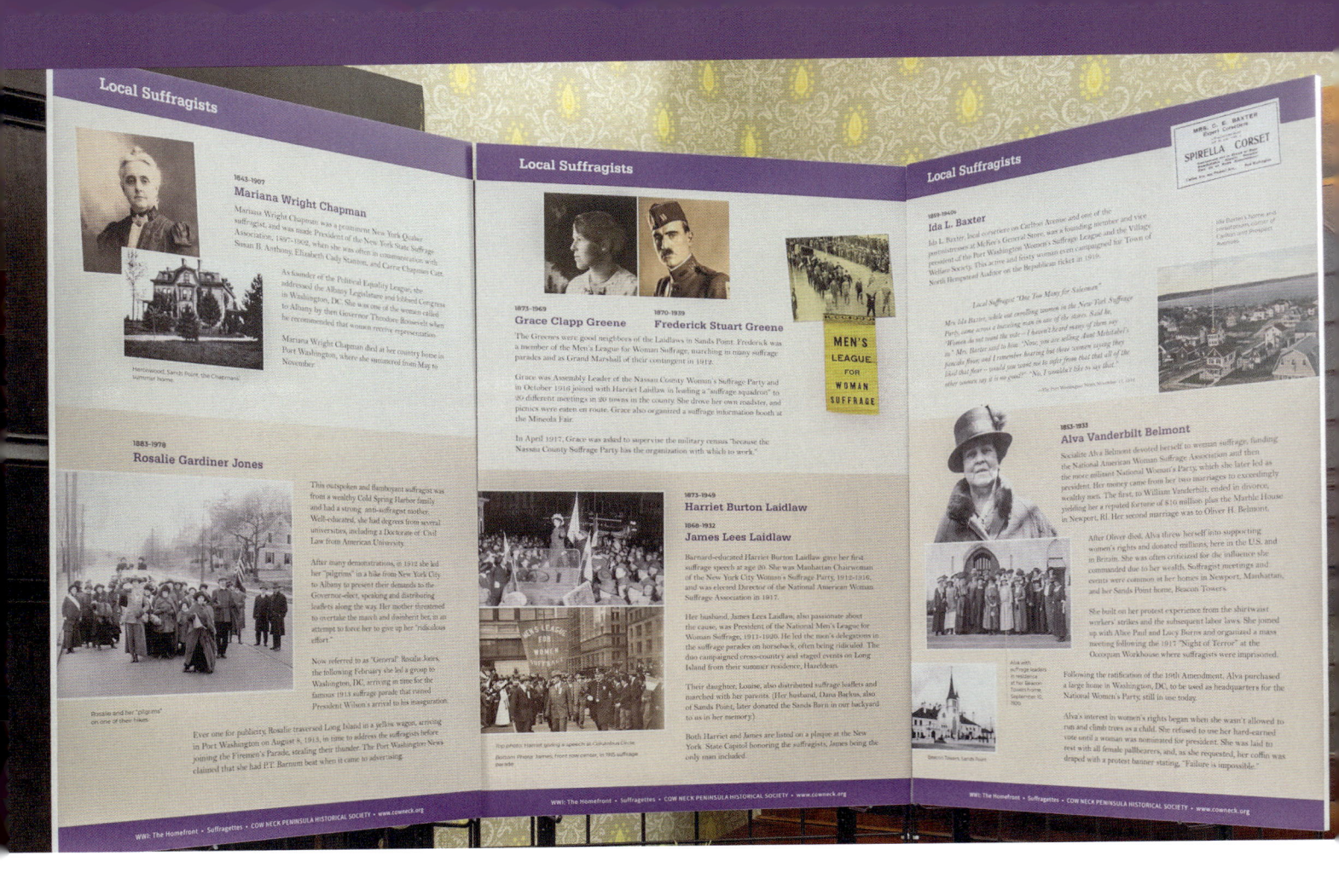

# Local Suffragists

Our community was active in their support of the suffragist movement from early on. Starting with the formation of the local branch of the Political Equality League in 1895 and followed by the North Hempstead Equal Suffrage League in 1913, it soon became a popular undertaking. Sands Point women who moved in other circles became influential on a national, state, island-wide, and community level. More local Port Washingtonians got involved with them in different organizations and led the way in setting up activities in town and planning events.

### 1859–1940s
# Ida L. Baxter

Ida L. Baxter, local corsetiere on Carlton Avenue and one of the postmistresses in town, was a founding member and vice president of the Port Washington Women's Suffrage League and the Village Welfare Society. This active and feisty woman even campaigned for Town of North Hempstead Auditor on the Republican ticket in 1919.

> *Local Suffragist "One Too Many for Salesman". Mrs. Ida Baxter, while out enrolling women in the New York Suffrage Party, came across a traveling man in one of the stores. Said he, "Women do not want the vote – I haven't heard many of them say so." Mrs. Baxter said to him: "Now, you are selling Aunt Mehitabel's pancake flour; and I remember hearing but three women saying they liked that flour – would you want me to infer from that that all of the other women say it is no good?" "No, I wouldn't like to say that."*
>
> —The Port Washington News, November 17, 1916

Ida Baxter's home and corsetorium, corner of Carlton and Prospect Avenues.

### 1843–1907
# Mariana Wright Chapman

Mariana Wright Chapman was a prominent New York Quaker suffragist and was made President of the New York State Suffrage Association, 1897-1902, when she was often in communication with Susan B. Anthony, Elizabeth Cady Stanton, and Carrie Chapman Catt.

As founder of the Political Equality League, she addressed the Albany Legislature and lobbied Congress in Washington, DC. She was one of the women called to Albany by then Governor Theodore Roosevelt when he recommended that women receive representation.

Mariana Wright Chapman died at her country home in Port Washington, where she summered from May to November.

Heronwood, Sands Point, the Chapmans' summer home.

WWI: The Homefront • Suffragettes • Cow Neck Peninsula Historical Society

#### 1853–1933
# Alva Vanderbilt Belmont

Socialite Alva Belmont devoted herself to woman suffrage, funding the National American Woman Suffrage Association and then the more militant National Woman's Party, which she later led as president. Her money came from her two marriages to exceedingly wealthy men. The first, to William Vanderbilt, ended in divorce, yielding her a reputed fortune of $10 million plus the Marble House in Newport, RI. Her second marriage was to Oliver H. Belmont.

After Oliver died, Alva threw herself into supporting women's rights and donated millions, here in the U.S. and in Britain. She was often criticized for the influence she commanded due to her wealth. Suffragist meetings and events were common at her homes in Newport, Manhattan, and her Sands Point home, Beacon Towers.

She built on her protest experience from the shirtwaist workers' strikes and the subsequent labor laws. She joined up with Alice Paul and Lucy Burns and organized a mass meeting following the 1917 "Night of Terror" at the Occoquan Workhouse where suffragettes were imprisoned.

Following the ratification of the 19th Amendment, Alva purchased a large home in Washington, DC, to be used as headquarters for the National Women's Party, still in use today.

Alva's interest in women's rights began when she wasn't allowed to run and climb trees as a child. She refused to use her hard-earned vote until a woman was nominated for president. She was laid to rest with all female pallbearers, and, as she requested, her coffin was draped with a protest banner stating, "Failure is impossible."

Alva with suffrage leaders in residence at her Beacon Towers home, in Sands Point, September 10, 1920.

**152** WWI: The Homefront • Suffragettes • Cow Neck Peninsula Historical Society

**1883–1978**

# Rosalie Gardiner Jones

This outspoken and flamboyant suffragist was from a wealthy Cold Spring Harbor family and had a strong anti-suffragist mother. Well-educated, she had degrees from several universities, including a Doctorate of Civil Law from American University.

After many demonstrations, in 1912 she led her "pilgrims" in a hike from New York City to Albany to present their demands to the Governor-elect, speaking and distributing leaflets along the way. Her mother threatened to overtake the march and disinherit her, in an attempt to force her to give up her "ridiculous effort."

Now referred to as "General" Rosalie Jones, the following February she led a group to Washington, DC, arriving in time for the famous 1913 suffrage parade that overshadowed President Wilson's arrival to his inauguration.

Ever one for publicity, Rosalie traversed Long Island in a yellow wagon, arriving in Port Washington on August 8, 1913, in time to address the suffragists before joining the Firemen's Parade, stealing their thunder. The Port Washington News claimed that she had P.T. Barnum beat when it came to advertising.

Rosalie and her "pilgrims" on one of their hikes.

1873–1969
# Grace Clapp Greene
1870–1939
# Frederick Stuart Greene

The Greenes were good neighbors of the Laidlaws in Sands Point. Frederick was a member of the Men's League for Woman Suffrage, marching in many suffrage parades and as Grand Marshal of their contingent in 1912.

Grace was Assembly Leader of the Nassau County Woman's Suffrage Party and in October 1916 joined with Harriet Laidlaw in leading a "suffrage squadron" to 20 different meetings in 20 towns in the county. She drove her own roadster, and picnics were eaten en route. Grace also organized a suffrage information booth at the Mineola Fair.

In April 1917, Grace was asked to supervise the military census "because the Nassau County Suffrage Party has the organization with which to work."

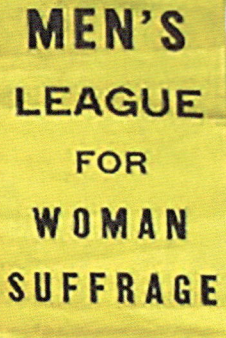

### 1873–1949
# Harriet Burton Laidlaw
### 1868–1932
# James Lees Laidlaw

Barnard-educated Harriet Burton Laidlaw gave her first suffrage speech at age 20. She was Manhattan Chairwoman of the New York City Woman's Suffrage Party, 1912-1916, and was elected Director of the National American Woman Suffrage Association in 1917.

Her husband, James Lees Laidlaw, also passionate about the cause, was President of the National Men's League for Woman Suffrage, 1911-1920. He led the men's delegations in the suffrage parades on horseback, often being ridiculed. The duo campaigned cross-country and staged events on Long Island from their summer residence, Hazeldean.

Their daughter, Louise, also distributed suffrage leaflets and marched with her parents. (Her husband, Dana Backus, also of Sands Point, later donated the Sands Barn in our backyard to us in her memory.)

Both Harriet and James are listed on a plaque at the New York State Capitol honoring the suffragists, James being the only man included.

**Top**: Harriet giving a speech at Columbus Circle.

**Bottom:** James, front row center, in 1915 suffrage parade.

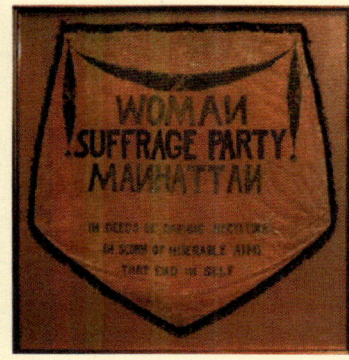

Courtesy of the Local History Center, Port Washington Public Library.

**Harriet Burton Laidlaw**, Manhattan Borough Chairwoman of the Woman Suffrage Party, with WOMAИ SUFFRAGE PARTY MAИHATTAИ banner, c. 1915.

It is not known why the И, a letter in the Russian or Cyrillic alphabet, was used.

The embroidery reads, "In deeds of daring rectitude, in scorn of miserable aims that end in self," from a poem, "The Choir Invisible," by George Eliot.

WWI: The Homefront • Suffragettes • Cow Neck Peninsula Historical Society

## The Willets Women

The Willets were the second family to give their name to our Sands-Willets House. Edmund Willets purchased the original Sands homestead and farm in 1845 and enlarged the house into the home it is today. Our Society purchased the home following the death of his last descendant living in the house, Miss Eliza Willets.

Eliza "Lila" and her sister Anna "Nana" lived in the house with their aunt, Anna "Aunty" Willets. They were active members of the Brooklyn Woman Suffrage Association. In 1901, Eliza and Aunty Anna attended the National Woman's Suffrage Association convention in Minneapolis,

**1834–1912**
### Anna Willets

**1873–1965**
### Eliza Willets

**1878–1956**
### Anna Willets Lapham

where Susan B. Anthony was a featured speaker. Eliza's diary revealed that they then joined other suffragists on a trip to Yellowstone Park.

Eliza's diary also reports that on February 10, 1904, "Aunty and Nan left at 8:30 am to Washington where they have gone to attend the Suffrage Convention." Anna returned from the annual convention of the Political Equality League with Mrs. Mariana Chapman where they had represented the Friends League of Port Washington.

Aunty Anna, in her 60s, seems to have been acting as chaperone to her single nieces who were in their 20s. All of them were active in the Village Welfare Society, which provided nursing care, sponsored canning kitchens, and supplied families in need.

**Eliza Willets**  **Anna Willets**  **Anna Willets Lapham**

# To All Who Served

# Thank you

Poppy Field.
(Photo: Bibi Jordan)